A

THEORY

of

HUMAN MOTIVATION

A.H. Maslow

Martino Publishing
Mansfield Centre, CT
2013

Martino Publishing
P.O. Box 373,
Mansfield Centre, CT 06250 USA

ISBN 978-1-61427-437-7

Cover design by T. Matarazzo

Printed in the United States of America On 100% Acid-Free Paper

A

THEORY

of

HUMAN MOTIVATION

A.H. Maslow

Originally Published in the
Psychological Review, 50(4), 370–96
1943

A Theory of Human Motivation*

A. H. MASLOW

I. INTRODUCTION

In a previous paper[1] various propositions were presented which would have to be included in any theory of human motivation that could lay claim to being definitive. These conclusions may be briefly summarized as follows:

1. The integrated wholeness of the organism must be one of the foundation stones of motivation theory.

2. The hunger drive (or any other physiological drive) was rejected as a centering point or model for a definitive theory of motivation. Any drive that is somatically based and localizable was shown to be atypical rather than typical in human motivation.

3. Such a theory should stress and center itself upon ultimate or basic goals rather than partial or superficial ones, upon ends rather than means to these ends. Such a stress would imply a more central place for unconscious than for conscious motivations.

4. There are usually available various cultural paths to the same goal. Therefore conscious, specific, local-cultural desires are not as fundamental in motivation theory as the more basic, unconscious goals.

5. Any motivated behavior, either preparatory or consummatory, must be understood to be a channel through which many basic needs may be simultaneously expressed or satisfied. Typically an act has *more* than one motivation.

6. Practically all organismic states are to be understood as motivated and as motivating.

7. Human needs arrange themselves in hierarchies of prepotency. That is to say, the appearance of one need usually rests on the prior satisfaction of another, more pre-potent need. Man is a perpetually wanting animal. Also no need or drive can be treated as if it were isolated or discrete; every drive is related to the state of satisfaction or dissatisfaction of other drives.

8. *Lists* of drives will get us nowhere for various theoretical and practical reasons. Furthermore any classification of motivations must deal with the problem of levels of specificity or generalization of the motives to be classified.

9. Classifications of motivations must be based upon goals rather than upon instigating drives or motivated behavior.

10. Motivation theory should be human-centered rather than animal-centered.

11. The situation or the field in which the organism reacts must be taken into account but the field alone can rarely serve as an exclusive explanation for behavior. Furthermore the field itself must be interpreted in terms of the organism. Field theory cannot be a substitute for motivation theory.

12. Not only the integration of the organism must be taken into account, but also the possibility of isolated, specific, partial or segmental reactions.

It has since become necessary to add to these another affirmation.

13. Motivations theory is not synonymous with behavior theory. The motivations are only one class of determinants of behavior. While behavior is almost always motivated, it is also almost always biologically, culturally and situationally determined as well.

The present paper is an attempt to formulate a positive theory of motivation which will satisfy these theoretical demands and at the same time conform

*Source: Psychological Review, vol. 50 (July 1943), pp. 370-396. Footnotes and pertinent references combined and renumbered; references not appearing in text have been omitted.

to the known facts, clinical and observational as well as experimental. It derives most directly, however, from clinical experience. This theory is, I think, in the functionalist tradition of James and Dewey, and is fused with the holism of Wertheimer,[2] Goldstein,[3] and Gestalt Psychology, and with the dynamicism of Freud[4] and Adler.[5] This fusion or synthesis may arbitrarily be called a "general-dynamic" theory.

It is far easier to perceive and to criticize the aspects in motivation theory than to remedy them. Mostly this is because of the very serious lack of sound data in this area. I conceive this lack of sound facts to be due primarily to the absence of a valid theory of motivation. The present theory then must be considered to be a suggested program or framework for future research and must stand or fall, not so much on facts available or evidence presented, as upon researches yet to be done, researches suggested perhaps, by the questions raised in this paper.

II. THE BASIC NEEDS

The "physiological" needs.—The needs that are usually taken as the starting point for motivation theory are the so-called physiological drives. Two recent lines of research make it necessary to revise our customary notions about these needs, first, the development of the concept of homeostasis, and second, the finding that appetites (preferential choices among foods) are a fairly efficient indication of actual needs or lacks in the body.

Homeostasis refers to the body's automatic efforts to maintain a constant, normal state of the blood stream. Cannon[6] has described this process for (1) the water content of the blood, (2) salt content, (3) sugar content, (4) protein content, (5) fat content, (6) calcium content, (7) oxygen content, (8) constant hydrogen-ion level (acid-base balance) and (9) constant temperature of the blood. Obviously this list can be ex-

tended to include other minerals, the hormones, vitamins, etc.

Young in a recent article[7] has summarized the work on appetite in its relation to body needs. If the body lacks some chemical, the individual will tend to develop a specific appetite or partial hunger for that food element.

Thus it seems impossible as well as useless to make any list of fundamental physiological needs for they can come to almost any number one might wish, depending on the degree of specificity of description. We can not identify all physiological needs as homeostatic. That sexual desire, sleepiness, sheer activity and maternal behavior in animals, are homeostatic, has not yet been demonstrated. Furthermore, this list would not include the various sensory pleasures (tastes, smells, tickling, stroking) which are probably physiological and which may become the goals of motivated behavior.

In a previous paper[8] it has been pointed out that these physiological drives or needs are to be considered unusual rather than typical because they are isolable, and because they are localizable somatically. That is to say, they are relatively independent of each other, of other motivations and of the organism as a whole, and secondly, in many cases, it is possible to demonstrate a localized, underlying somatic base for the drive. This is true less generally than has been thought (exceptions are fatigue, sleepiness, maternal responses) but it is till true in the classic instances of hunger, sex, and thirst.

It should be pointed out again that any of the physiological needs and the consummatory behavior involved with them serve as channels for all sorts of other needs as well. That is to say, the person who thinks he is hungry may actually be seeking more for comfort, or dependence, than for vitamins or proteins. Conversely, it is possible to satisfy the hunger need in part by other activities such as drinking water or smoking cigarettes. In other words, relatively isolable as these physiological needs are, they are not completely so.

Undoubtedly these physiological needs are the most prepotent of all needs. What this means specifically is, that in the human being who is missing everything in life in an extreme fashion, it is most likely that the major motivation would be the physiological needs rather than any others. A person who is lacking food, safety, love, and esteem would most probably hunger for food more strongly than for anything else.

If all the needs are unsatisfied, and the organism is then dominated by the physiological needs, all other needs may become simply non-existent or be pushed into the background. It is then fair to characterize the whole organism by saying simply that it is hungry, for consciousness is almost completely preempted by hunger. All capacities are put into the service of hunger-satisfaction, and the organization of these capacities is almost entirely determined by the one purpose of satisfying hunger. The receptors and effectors, the intelligence, memory, habits, all may now be defined simply as hunger-gratifying tools. Capacities that are not useful for this purpose lie dormant, or are pushed into the background. The urge to write poetry, the desire to acquire an automobile, the interest in American history, the desire for a new pair of shoes are, in the extreme case, forgotten or become of secondary importance. For the man who is extremely and dangerously hungry, no other interests exist but food. He dreams food, he remembers food, he thinks about food, he emotes only about food, he perceives only food and he wants only food. The more subtle determinants that ordinarily fuse with the physiological drives in organizing even feeding, drinking or sexual behavior, may now be so completely overwhelmed as to allow us to speak at this time (but *only* at this time) of pure hunger drive and behavior, with the one unqualified aim of relief.

Another peculiar characteristic of the human organism when it is dominated by a certain need is that the whole philosophy of the future tends also to change. For our chronically and extremely hungry man, Utopia can be defined very simply as a place where there is plenty of food. He tends to think that, if only he is guaranteed food for the rest of his life, he will be perfectly happy and will never want anything more. Life itself tends to be defined in terms of eating. Anything else will be defined as unimportant. Freedom, love, community feeling, respect, philosophy, may all be waved aside as fripperies which are useless since they fail to fill the stomach. Such a man may fairly be said to live by bread alone.

It cannot possibly be denied that such things are true but their *generality* can be denied. Emergency conditions are, almost by definition, rare in the normally functioning peaceful society. That this truism can be forgotten is due mainly to two reasons. First, rats have few motivations other than physiological ones, and since so much of the research upon motivation has been made with these animals, it is easy to carry the rat-picture over to the human being. Secondly, it is too often not realized that culture itself is an adaptive tool, one of whose main functions is to make the physiological emergencies come less and less often. In most of the known societies, chronic extreme hunger of the emergency type is rare, rather than common. In any case, this is till true in the United States. The average American citizen is experiencing appetite rather than hunger when he says "I am hungry." He is apt to experience sheer life-and-death hunger only by accident and then only a few times through his entire life.

Obviously a good way to obscure the "higher" motivations, and to get a lopsided view of human capacities and human nature, is to make the organism extremely and chronically hungry or thirsty. Anyone who attempts to make an emergency picture into a typical one, and who will measure all of man's goals and desires by his behavior during extreme physiological deprivation is certainly being blind to many things. It is quite true that man lives by bread alone—when there is no bread. But what happens to man's desires when there *is* plenty of bread and when his belly is chronically filled?

At once other (and "higher") needs emerge and these, rather than physiological hungers, dominate the organism. And when these in turn are satisfied, again new (and still "higher") needs emerge and so on. This is what we mean by saying that the basic human needs are organized into a hierarchy of relative prepotency.

One main implication of this phrasing is that gratification becomes as important a concept as deprivation in motivation theory, for it releases the organism from the domination of a relatively more physiological need, permitting thereby the emergence of other more social goals. The physiological needs, along with their partial goals, when chronically gratified cease to exist as active determinants or organizers of behavior. They now exist only in a potential fashion in the sense that they may emerge again to dominate the organism if they are thwarted. But a want that is satisfied is no longer a want. The organism is dominated and its behavior organized only by unsatisfied needs. If hunger is satisfied, it becomes unimportant in the current dynamics of the individual.

This statement is somewhat qualified by a hypothesis to be discussed more fully later, namely that it is precisely those individuals in whom a certain need has always been satisfied who are best equipped to tolerate deprivation of that need in the future, and that furthermore, those who have been deprived in the past will react differently to current satisfactions than the one who has never been deprived.

The safety needs.—If the physiological needs are relatively well gratified, there then emerges a new set of needs, which we may categorize roughly as the safety needs. All that has been said of the physiological needs is equally true, although in lesser degree, of these desires. The organism may equally well be wholly dominated by them. They may serve as the almost exclusive organizers of behavior, recruiting all the capacities of the organism in their service, and we may then fairly describe the whole organism as a safety-seeking mechanism. Again we may say of the receptors, the effectors, of the intellect and the other capacities that they are primarily safety-seeking tools. Again, as in the hungry man, we find that the dominating goal is a strong determinant not only of his current world-outlook and philosophy but also of his philosophy of the future. Practically everything looks less important than safety, (even sometimes the physiological needs which being satisfied, are now underestimated). A man, in this state, if it is extreme enough and chronic enough, may be characterized as living almost for safety alone.

Although in this paper we are interested primarily in the needs of the adult, we can approach an understanding of his safety needs perhaps more efficiently by observation of infants and children, in whom these needs are much more simple and obvious. One reason for the clearer appearance of the threat or danger reaction in infants, is that they do not inhibit this reaction at all, whereas adults in our society have been taught to inhibit it at all costs. Thus even when adults do feel their safety to be threatened we may not be able to see this on the surface. Infants will react in a total fashion and as if they were endangered, if they are disturbed or dropped suddenly, startled by loud noises, flashing light, or other unusual sensory stimulation, by rough handling, by general loss of support in the mother's arms, or by inadequate support.[9]

4

In infants we can also see a much more direct reaction to bodily illnesses of various kinds. Sometimes these illnesses seem to be immediately and *per se* threatening and seem to make the child feel unsafe. For instance, vomiting, colic or other sharp pains seem to make the child look at the whole world in a different way. At such a moment of pain, it may be postulated that, for the child, the appearance of the whole world suddenly changes from sunniness to darkness, so to speak, and becomes a place in which anything at all might happen, in which previously stable things have suddenly become unstable. Thus a child who because of some bad food is taken ill may, for a day or two, develop fear, nightmares, and a need for protection and reassurance never seen in him before his illness.

Another indication of the child's need for safety is his preference for some kind of undisrupted routine or rhythm. He seems to want a predictable, orderly world. For instance, injustice, unfairness, or inconsistency in the parents seems to make a child feel anxious and unsafe. This attitude may be not so much because of the injustice *per se* or any particular pains involved, but rather because this treatment threatens to make the world look unreliable, or unsafe, or unpredictable. Young children seem to thrive better under a system which has at least a skeletal outline of rigidity, in which there is a schedule of a kind, some sort of routine, something that can be counted upon, not only for the present but also far into the future. Perhaps one could express this more accurately by saying that the child needs an organized world rather than an unorganized or unstructured one.

The central role of the parents and the normal family setup are indisputable. Quarreling, physical assault, separation, divorce or death within the family may be particularly terrifying. Also parental outbursts of rage or threats of punishment directed to the child, calling him names, speaking to him harshly, shaking him, handling him roughly, or actual physical punishment sometimes elicit such total panic and terror in the child that we must assume more is involved than the physical pain alone. While it is true that in some children this terror may represent also a fear of loss of parental love, it can also occur in completely rejected children, who seem to cling to the hating parents more for sheer safety and protection than because of hope of love.

Confronting the average child with new, unfamiliar, strange, unmanageable stimuli or situations will too frequently elicit the danger or terror reaction, as for example, getting lost or even being separated from the parents for a short time, being confronted with new faces, new situations or new tasks, the sight of strange, unfamiliar or uncontrollable objects, illness or death. Particularly at such times, the child's frantic clinging to his parents is eloquent testimony to their role as protectors (quite apart from their roles as food-givers and love-givers).

From these and similar observations, we may generalize and say that the average child in our society generally prefers a safe, orderly, predictable, organized world, which he can count on, and in which unexpected, unmanageable or other dangerous things do not happen, and in which, in any case, he has all-powerful parents who protect and shield him from harm.

That these reactions may so easily be observed in children is in a way a proof of the fact that children in our society, feel too unsafe (or, in a word, are badly brought up). Children who are reared in an unthreatening, loving family do *not* ordinarily react as we have described above.[10] In such children the danger reactions are apt to come mostly to objects or situations that adults too would consider dangerous.[11]

The healthy, normal, fortunate adult in our culture is largely satisfied in his safety needs. The peaceful, smoothly running, "good" society ordinarily makes its members feel safe enough from wild animals, extremes of temperature, criminals, assault and murder, tyranny, etc. Therefore, in a very real sense, he no longer has any safety needs as active motivators. Just as a sated man no longer feels hungry, a safe man no longer feels endangered. If we wish to see these needs directly and clearly we must turn to neurotic or near-neurotic individuals, and to the economic and social underdogs. In between these extremes, we can perceive the expressions of safety needs only in such phenomena as, for instance, the common preference for a job with tenure and protection, the desire for a savings account, and for insurance of various kinds (medical, dental, unemployment, disability, old age).

Other broader aspects of the attempt to seek safety and stability in the world are seen in the very common preference for familiar rather than unfamiliar things, or for the known rather than the unknown. The tendency to have some religion or world-philosophy that organizes the universe and the men in it into some sort of satisfactorily coherent, meaningful whole is also in part motivated by safety-seeking. Here too we may list science and philosophy in general as partially motivated by the safety needs (we shall see later that there are also other motivations to scientific, philosophical or religious endeavor).

Otherwise the need for safety is seen as an active and dominant mobilizer of the organism's resources only in emergencies, e.g., war, disease, natural catastrophes, crime waves, societal disorganization, neurosis, brain injury, chronically bad situation.

Some neurotic adults in our society are, in many ways, like the unsafe child in their desire for safety, although in the former it takes on a somewhat special appearance. Their reaction is often to unknown, psychological dangers in a world that is perceived to be hostile, overwhelming and threatening. Such a person behaves as if a great catastrophe were almost always impending, i.e., he is usually responding as if to an emergency. His safety needs often find specific expression in a search for a protector, or a stronger person on whom he may depend, or perhaps, a Fuehrer.

The neurotic individual may be described in a slightly different way with some usefulness as a grown-up person who retains his childish attitudes toward the world. That is to say, a neurotic adult may be said to behave "as if" he were actually afraid of a spanking, or of his mother's disapproval, or of being abandoned by his parents, or having his food taken away from him. It is as if his childish attitudes of fear and threat reaction to a dangerous world had gone underground, and untouched by the growing up and learning processes, were now ready to be called out by any stimulus that would make a child feel endangered and threatened.[12]

The neurosis in which the search for safety takes its clearest form is in the compulsive-obsessive neurosis. Compulsive-obsessives try frantically to order and stabilize the world so that no unmanageable, unexpected or unfamiliar dangers will ever appear.[13] They hedge themselves about with all sorts of ceremonials, rules and formulas so that every possible contingency may be provided for and so that no new contingencies may appear. They are much like the brain injured cases, described by Goldstein,[14] who manage to maintain their equilibrium by avoiding everything unfamiliar and strange and by ordering their restricted world in such a neat, disciplined, orderly fashion that everything in the world can be counted upon. They try to arrange the world so that anything unexpected (dangers) cannot possibly occur. If, through no fault of their own, something unexpected does occur, they go into a panic reaction as if this unexpected occurrence constituted a grave danger. What we can see only as a none-too-strong preference in the healthy person, e.g., preference for the familiar, becomes a life-and-death necessity in abnormal cases.

The love needs.—If both the

physiological and the safety needs are fairly well gratified, then there will emerge the love and affection and belongingness needs, and the whole cycle already described will repeat itself with this new center. Now the person will feel keenly, as never before, the absence of friends, or a sweetheart, or a wife, or children. He will hunger for affectionate relations with people in general, namely, for a place in his group, and he will strive with great intensity to achieve this goal. He will want to attain such a place more than anything else in the world and may even forget that once, when he was hungry, he sneered at love.

In our society the thwarting of these needs is the most commonly found core in cases of maladjustment and more severe psychopathology. Love and affection, as well as their possible expression in sexuality, are generally looked upon with ambivalence and are customarily hedged about with many restrictions and inhibitions. Practically all theorists of psychopathology have stressed thwarting of the love needs as basic in the picture of maladjustment. Many clinical studies have therefore been made of this need and we know more about it perhaps than any of the other needs except the physiological ones.[15]

One thing that must be stressed at this point is that love is not synonymous with sex. Sex may be studied as a purely physiological need. Ordinarily sexual behavior is multi-determined, that is to say, determined not only by sexual but also by other needs, chief among which are the love and affection needs. Also not to be overlooked is the fact that the love needs involve both giving *and* receiving love.[16]

The esteem needs.—All people in our society (with a few pathological exceptions) have a need or desire for a stable, firmly based, (usually) high evaluation of themselves, for self-respect, or self-esteem, and for the esteem of others. By firmly based self-esteem, we mean that which is soundly based upon real capacity, achievement and respect from others. These needs may be classified into two subsidiary sets. These are, first, the desire for strength, for achievement, for adequacy, for confidence in the face of the world, and for independence and freedom.[17] Secondly, we have what we may call the desire for reputation or prestige (defining it as respect or esteem from other people), recognition, attention, importance or appreciation.[18] These needs have been relatively stressed by Alfred Adler and his followers, and have been relatively neglected by Freud and the psychoanalysts. More and more today however there is appearing widespread appreciation of their central importance.

Satisfaction of the self-esteem need leads to feelings of self-confidence, worth, strength, capability and adequacy of being useful and necessary in the world. But thwarting of these needs produces feelings of inferiority, of weakness and of helplessness. These feelings in turn give rise to either basic discouragement or else compensatory or neurotic trends. An appreciation of the necessity of basic self-confidence and an understanding of how helpless people are without it, can be easily gained from a study of severe traumatic neurosis.[19]

The need for self-actualization.—Even if all these needs are satisfied, we may still often (if not always) expect that a new discontent and restlessness will soon develop, unless the individual is doing what he is fitted for. A musician must make music, an artist must paint, a poet must write, if he is to be ultimately happy. What a man *can* be, he *must* be. This need we may call self-actualization.

This term, first coined by Kurt Goldstein, is being used in this paper in a much more specific and limited fashion. It refers to the desire for self-fulfillment, namely, to the tendency for him to become actualized in what he is potentially. This tendency might be phrased as the desire to become more and more what one is, to become everything that one is capable of becoming.

The specific form that these needs will take will of course vary greatly from person to person. In one individual it may take the form of the desire to be an ideal mother, in another it may be expressed athletically, and in still another it may be expressed in painting pictures or in inventions. It is not necessarily a creative urge although in people who have any capacities for creation it will take this form.

The clear emergence of these needs rests upon prior satisfaction of the physiological, safety, love and esteem needs. We shall call people who are satisfied in these needs, basically satisfied people, and it is from these that we may expect the fullest (and healthiest) creativeness.[20] Since, in our society, basically satisfied people are the exception, we do not know much about self-actualization, either experimentally or clinically. It remains a challenging problem for research.

The preconditions for the basic need satisfactions.—There are certain conditions which are immediate prerequisites for the basic need satisfactions. Danger to these is reacted to almost as if it were a direct danger to the basic needs themselves. Such conditions as freedom to speak, freedom to do what one wishes so long as no harm is done to others, freedom to express one's self, freedom to investigate and seek for information, freedom to defend one's self, justice, fairness, honesty, orderliness in the group are examples of such preconditions for basic need satisfactions. Thwarting in these freedoms will be reacted to with a threat or emergency response. These conditions are not ends in themselves but they are *almost* so since they are so closely related to the basic needs, which are apparently the only ends in themselves. These conditions are defended because without them the basic satisfactions are quite impossible, or at least, very severely endangered.

If we remember that the cognitive capacities (perceptual, intellectual, learning) are a set of adjustive tools, which have, among other functions, that of satisfaction of our basic needs, then it is clear that any danger to them, any deprivation or blocking of their free use, must also be indirectly threatening to the basic needs themselves. Such a statement is a partial solution of the general problems of curiosity, the search for knowledge, truth and wisdom, and the ever-persistent urge to solve the cosmic mysteries.

We must therefore introduce another hypothesis and speak of degrees of closeness to the basic needs, for we have already pointed out that any conscious desires (partial goals) are more or less important as they are more or less close to the basic needs. The same statement may be made for various behavior acts. An act is psychologically important if it contributes directly to satisfaction of basic needs. The less directly it so contributes, or the weaker this contribution is, the less important this act must be conceived to be from the point of view of dynamic psychology. A similar statement may be made for the various defense or coping mechanisms. Some are very directly related to the protection or attainment of the basic needs, others are only weakly and distantly related. Indeed if we wished, we could speak of more basic and less basic defense mechanisms, and then affirm that danger to the more basic defenses is more threatening than danger to less basic defenses (always remembering that this is so only because of their relationship to the basic needs).

The desires to know and to understand.—So far, we have mentioned the cognitive needs only in passing. Acquiring knowledge and systematizing the universe have been considered as, in part, techniques for the achievement of basic safety in the world, or, for the intelligent man, expressions of self-actualization. Also freedom of inquiry and expression have been discussed as preconditions of satisfactions of the basic needs. True though these formulations may be, they do not constitute definitive answers to the question as to the motivation role of curiosity, learning, philosophizing, experimenting, etc. They are, at best, no more than partial answers.

This question is especially difficult because we know so little about the facts. Curiosity, exploration, desire for the facts, desire to know may certainly be observed easily enough. The fact that they often are pursued even at great cost to the individual's safety is an earnest of the partial character of our previous discussion. In addition, the writer must admit that, though he has sufficient clinical evidence to postulate the desire to know as a very strong drive in intelligent people, no data are available for unintelligent people. It may then be largely a function of relatively high intelligence. Rather tentatively, then, and largely in the hope of stimulating discussion and research, we shall postulate a basic desire to know, to be aware of reality, to get the facts, to satisfy curiosity, or as Wertheimer phrases it, to see rather than to be blind.

This postulation, however, is not enough. Even after we know, we are impelled to know more and more minutely and microscopically on the one hand, and on the other, more and more extensively in the direction of world philosophy, religion, etc. The facts that we acquire, if they are isolated or atomistic, inevitably get theorized about, and either analyzed or organized or both. This process has been phrased by some as the search for "meaning." We shall then postulate a desire to understand, to systematize, to organize, to analyze, to look for relations and meanings.

Once these desires are accepted for discussion, we see that they too form themselves into a small hierarchy in which the desire to know is prepotent over the desire to understand. All the characteristics of a hierarchy of prepotency that we have described above, seem to hold for this one as well.

We must guard ourselves against the too easy tendency to separate these desires from the basic needs we have discussed above, i.e., to make a sharp dichotomy between "cognitive" and "conative" needs. The desire to know and to understand are themselves conative, i.e., have a striving character, and are as much personality needs as the "basic needs" we have already discussed.[21]

III. FURTHER CHARACTERISTICS OF THE BASIC NEEDS

The degree of fixity of the hierarchy of basic needs.—We have spoken so far as if this hierarchy were a fixed order but actually it is not nearly as rigid as we may have implied. It is true that most of the people with whom we have worked have seemed to have these basic needs in about the order that has been indicated. However, there have been a number of exceptions.

(1) There are some people in whom, for instance, self-esteem seems to be more important than love. This most common reversal in the hierarchy is usually due to the development of the notion that the person who is most likely to be loved is a strong or powerful person, one who inspires respect or fear, and who is self confident or aggressive. Therefore such people who lack love and seek it, may try hard to put on a front of aggressive, confident behavior. But essentially they seek high self-esteem and its behavior expressions more as a means-to-an-end than for its own sake; they seek self-assertion for the sake of love rather than for self-esteem itself.

(2) There are other, apparently innately creative people in whom the drive to creativeness seems to be more important than any other counterdeterminant. Their creativeness might

appear not as self-actualization released by basic satisfaction, but in spite of lack of basic satisfaction.

(3) In certain people the level of aspiration may be permanently deadened or lowered. That is to say, the less prepotent goals may simply be lost, and may disappear forever, so that the person who has experienced life at a very low level, i.e., chronic unemployment, may continue to be satisfied for the rest of his life if only he can get enough food.

(4) The so-called "psychopathic personality" is another example of permanent loss of the love needs. These are people who, according to the best data available,[22] have been starved for love in the earliest months of their lives and have simply lost forever the desire and the ability to give and to receive affection (as animals lose sucking or pecking reflexes that are not exercised soon enough after birth).

(5) Another cause of reversal of the hierarchy is that when a need has been satisfied for a long time, this need may be underevaluated. People who have never experienced chronic hunger are apt to underestimate its effects and to look upon food as a rather unimportant thing. If they are dominated by a higher need, this higher need will seem to be the most important of all. It then becomes possible, and indeed does actually happen, that they may, for the sake of this higher need, put themselves into the position of being deprived in a more basic need. We may expect that after a long-time deprivation of the more basic need there will be a tendency to reevaluate both needs so that the more prepotent need will actually become consciously prepotent for the individual who may have given it up very lightly. Thus, a man who has given up his job rather than lose his self-respect, and who then starves for six months or so, may be willing to take his job back even at the price of losing his self-respect.

(6) Another partial explanation of *apparent* reversals is seen in the fact that we have been talking about the hierarchy of prepotency in terms of consciously felt wants or desires rather than of behavior. Looking at behavior itself may give us the wrong impression. What we have claimed is that the person will *want* the more basic of two needs when deprived in both. There is no necessary implication here that he will act upon his desires. Let us say again that there are many determinants of behavior other than the needs and desires.

(7) Perhaps more important than all these exceptions are the ones that involve ideals, high social standards, high values and the like. With such values people become martyrs; they will give up everything for the sake of a particular ideal, or value. These people may be understood, at least in part, by reference to one basic concept (or hypothesis) which may be called "increased frustration-tolerance through early gratification." People who have been satisfied in their basic needs throughout their lives, particularly in their earlier years, seem to develop exceptional power to withstand present or future thwarting of these needs simply because they have strong, healthy character structure as a result of basic satisfaction. They are the "strong" people who can easily weather disagreement or opposition, who can swim against the stream of public opinion and who can stand up for the truth at great personal cost. It is just the ones who have loved and been well loved, and who have had many deep friendships who can hold out against hatred, rejection or persecution.

I say all this in spite of the fact that there is a certain amount of sheer habituation which is also involved in any full discussion of frustration tolerance. For instance, it is likely that those persons who have been accustomed to relative starvation for a long time, are partially enabled thereby to withstand food deprivation. What sort of balance must be made between these two tendencies, of habituation on the one hand, and of past satisfaction breeding present frustration tolerance on the other hand, remains to be worked out by further research. Meanwhile we may assume that they are both operative, side by side, since they do not contradict each other. In respect to this phenomenon of increased frustration tolerance, it seems probable that the most important gratifications come in the first two years of life. That is to say, people who have been made secure and strong in the earliest years, tend to remain secure and strong thereafter in the face of whatever threatens.

Degrees of relative satisfaction.—So far, our theoretical discussion may have given the impression that these five sets of needs are somehow in a step-wise, all-or-none relationships to each other. We have spoken in such terms as the following: "If one need is satisfied, then another emerges." This statement might give the false impression that a need must be satisfied 100 per cent before the next need emerges. In actual fact, most members of our society who are normal, are partially satisfied in all their basic needs and partially unsatisfied in all their basic needs at the same time. A more realistic description of the hierarchy would be in terms of decreasing percentages of satisfaction as we go up the hierarchy of prepotency. For instance, if I may assign arbitrary figures for the sake of illustration, it is as if the average citizen is satisfied perhaps 85 per cent in his physiological needs, 70 per cent in his safety needs, 50 per cent in his love needs, 40 per cent in his self-esteem needs, and 10 per cent in his self-actualization needs.

As for the concept of emergence of a new need after satisfaction of the prepotent need, this emergence is not a sudden, saltatory phenomenon but rather a gradual emergence by slow degrees from nothingness. For instance, if prepotent need A is satisfied only 10 per cent then need B may not be visible at all. However, as this need A becomes satis-fied 25 per cent, need B may emerge 5 per cent, as need A becomes satisfied 75 per cent need B may emerge 90 per cent, and so on.

Unconscious character of needs.— These needs are neither necessarily conscious nor unconscious. On the whole, however, in the average person, they are more often unconscious rather than conscious. It is not necessary at this point to overhaul the tremendous mass of evidence which indicates the crucial importance of unconscious motivation. It would by now be expected, on a priori grounds alone, that unconscious motivations would on the whole be rather more important than the conscious motivations. What we have called the basic needs are very often largely unconscious although they may, with suitable techniques, and with sophisticated people become conscious.

Cultural specificity and generality of needs.—This classification of basic needs makes some attempt to take account of the relative unity behind the superficial differences in specific desires from one culture to another. Certainly in any particular culture an individual's conscious motivational content will usually be extremely different from the conscious motivational content of an individual in another society. However, it is the common experience of anthropologists that people, even in different societies, are much more alike than we would think from our first contact with them, and that as we know them better we seem to find more and more of this commonness. We then recognize the most startling differences to be superficial rather than basic, e.g., differences in style of hairdress, clothes, tastes in food, etc. Out classification of basic needs is in part an attempt to account for this unity behind the apparent diversity from culture to culture. No claim is made that it is ultimate or universal for all cultures. The claim is made only that it is relatively *more* ultimate, more universal, more basic, than the superficial conscious desires from culture to culture, and makes a somewhat closer approach to common-human characteristics. Basic needs are *more* common-human than superficial desires or behaviors.

Multiple motivations of behavior.— These needs must be understood *not* to be *exclusive* or single determiners of certain kinds of behavior. An example may be found in any behavior that seems to be physiologically motivated, such as eating, or sexual play or the like. The clinical psychologists have long since found that any behavior may be a channel through which flow various determinants. Or to say it in another way, most behavior is multi-motivated. Within the sphere of motivational determinants any behavior tends to be determined by several or *all* of the basic needs simultaneously rather than by only one of them. The latter would be more an exception than the former. Eating may be partially for the sake of filling the stomach, and partially for the sake of comfort and amelioration of other needs. One may make love not only for pure sexual release, but also to convince one's self of one's masculinity, or to make a conquest, to feel powerful, or to win more basic affection. As an illustration, I may point out that it would be possible (theoretically if not practically) to analyze a single act of an individual and see in it the expression of his physiological needs, his safety needs, his love needs, his esteem needs and self-actualization. This contrasts sharply with the more naive brand of trait psychology in which one trait or one motive accounts for a certain kind of act, *i.e.*, an aggressive act is traced solely to a trait of aggressiveness.

Multiple determinants of behavior.—Not all behavior is determined by the basic needs. We might even say that not all behavior is motivated. There are many determinants of behavior other than motives.[23] For instance, one other important class of determinants is the so-called "field" determinants. Theoretically, at least, behavior may be deter-

mined completely by the field, or even by specific isolated external stimuli, as in association of ideas, or certain conditioned reflexes. If in response to the stimulus word "table," I immediately perceive a memory image of a table, this response certainly has nothing to do with my basic needs.

Secondly, we may call attention again to the concept of "degree of closeness to the basic needs" or "degree of motivation." Some behavior is highly motivated, other behavior is only weakly motivated. Some is not motivated at all (but all behavior is determined).

Another important point[24] is that there is a basic difference between expressive behavior and coping behavior (functional striving, purposive goal seeking). An expressive behavior does not try to do anything; it is simply a reflection of the personality. A stupid man behaves stupidly, not because he wants to, or tries to, or is motivated to, but simply because he *is* what he is. The same is true when I speak in a bass voice rather than tenor or soprano. The random movements of a healthy child, the smile on the face of a happy man even when he is alone, the springiness of the healthy man's walk, and the erectness of his carriage are other examples of expressive, non-functional behavior. Also the *style* in which a man carries out almost all his behavior, motivated as well as unmotivated, is often expressive.

We may then ask, is *all* behavior expressive or reflective of the character structure? The answer is "No." Rote, habitual, automatized, or conventional behavior may or may not be expressive. The same is true for most "stimulus-bound" behaviors.

It is finally necessary to stress that expressiveness of behavior, and goal-directedness of behavior are not mutually exclusive categories. Average behavior is usually both.

Goals as centering principle in motivation theory.—It will be observed that the basic principle in our classification has been neither the instigation nor the motivated behavior but rather the functions, effects, purposes, or goals of the behavior. It has been proven sufficiently by various people that this is the most suitable point for centering in any motivation theory.[25]

Animal- and human-centering.—This theory starts with the human being rather than any lower and presumably "simpler" animal. Too many of the findings that have been made in animals have been proven to be true for animals but not for the human being. There is no reason whatsoever why we should start with animals in order to study human motivation. The logic or rather illogic behind this general fallacy of "pseudo-simplicity" has been exposed often enough by philosophers and logicians as well as by scientists in each of the various fields. It is no more necessary to study animals before one can study man than it is to study mathematics before one can study geology or psychology or biology.

We may also reject the old, naive, behaviorism which assumed that it was somehow necessary, or at least more "scientific" to judge human beings by animal standards. One consequence of this belief was that the whole notion of purpose and goal was excluded from motivational psychology simply because one could not ask a white rat about his purposes. Tolman[26] has long since proven in animal studies themselves that this exclusion was not necessary.

Motivation and the theory of psychopathogenesis.—The conscious motivational content of everyday life has, according to the foregoing, been conceived to be relatively important or unimportant accordingly as it is more or less closely related to the basic goals. A desire for an ice cream cone might actually be an indirect expression of a desire for love. If it is, then this desire for the ice cream cone becomes extremely important motivation. If however the ice cream is simply something to cool the mouth with, or a casual appetitive reac-

tion, then the desire is relatively unimportant. Everyday conscious desires are to be regarded as symptoms, as *surface indicators of more basic needs*. If we were to take these superficial desires at their face value we would find ourselves in a state of complete confusion which could never be resolved, since we would be dealing seriously with symptoms rather than with what lay behind the symptoms.

Thwarting of unimportant desires produces no psychopathological results; thwarting of a basically important need does produce such results. Any theory of psychopathogenesis must then be based on a sound theory of motivation. A conflict or a frustration is not necessarily pathogenic. It becomes so only when it threatens or thwarts the basic needs, or partial needs that are closely related to the basic needs.[27]

The role of gratified needs.—It has been pointed out above several times that our needs usually emerge only when more prepotent needs have been gratified. Thus gratification has an important role in motivation theory. Apart from this, however, needs cease to play an active determining or organizing role as soon as they are gratified.

What this means is that, e.g., a basically satisfied person no longer has the needs for esteem, love, safety, etc. The only sense in which he might be said to have them is in the almost metaphysical sense that a sated man has hunger, or a filled bottle has emptiness. If we are interested in what *actually* motivates us, and not in what has, will, or might motivate us, then a satisfied need is not a motivator. It must be considered for all practical purposes simply not to exist, to have disappeared. This point should be emphasized because it has been either overlooked or contradicted in every theory of motivation I know.[28] The perfectly healthy, normal, fortunate man has no sex needs or hunger needs, or needs for safety, or for love, or for prestige, or self-esteem, except in stray moments of quickly passing threat. If we were to say otherwise, we should also have to aver that every man had all the pathological reflexes, e.g., Babinski, etc., because if his nervous system were damaged, these would appear.

It is such considerations as these that suggest the bold postulation that a man who is thwarted in any of his basic needs may fairly be envisaged simply as a sick man. This is a fair parallel to our designation as "sick" of the man who lacks vitamins or minerals. Who is to say that a lack of love is less important than a lack of vitamins? Since we know the pathogenic effects of love starvation, who is to say that we are invoking value-questions in an unscientific or illegitimate way, any more than the physician does who diagnoses and treats pellagra or scurvy? If I were permitted this usage, I should then say simply that a healthy man is primarily motivated by his needs to develop and actualize his fullest potentialities and capacities. If a man has any other basic needs in any active, chronic sense, then he is simply an unhealthy man. He is as surely sick as if he had suddenly developed a strong salt-hunger or calcium hunger.[29]

If this statement seems unusual or paradoxical the reader may be assured that this is only one among many such paradoxes that will appear as we revise our ways of looking at man's deeper motivations. When we ask what man wants of life, we deal with his very essence.

IV. SUMMARY

(1) *There are at least five sets of goals, which we may call basic needs.* These are briefly physiological, safety, love, esteem, and self-actualization. In addition, we are motivated by the desire to achieve or maintain the various conditions upon which these basic satisfactions rest and by certain more intellectual desires.

(2) *These basic goals are related to each other, being arranged in a hierar-* chy of prepotency. This means that the most prepotent goal will monopolize consciousness and will tend of itself to organize the recruitment of the various capacities of the organism. The less prepotent needs are minimized, even forgotten or denied. But when a need is fairly well satisfied, the next prepotent ("higher") need emerges, in turn to dominate the conscious life and to serve as the center of organization of behavior, since gratified needs are not active motivators.

Thus man is a perpetually wanting animal. Ordinarily the satisfaction of these wants is not altogether mutually exclusive, but only tends to be. The average member of our society is most often partially satisfied and partially unsatisfied in all of his wants. The hierarchy principle is usually empirically observed in terms of increasing percentages of non-satisfaction as we go up the hierarchy. Reversals of the average order of the hierarchy are sometimes observed. Also it has been observed that an individual may permanently lose the higher wants in the hierarchy under special conditions. There are not only ordinarily multiple motivations for usual behavior, but in addition many determinants other than motives.

(3) *Any thwarting or possibility of thwarting of these basic human goals, or danger to the defenses which protect them, or to the conditions upon which they rest, is considered to be a psychological threat.* With a few exceptions, all psychopathology may be partially traced to such threats. A basically thwarted man may actually be defined as a "sick" man, if we wish.

(4) *It is such basic threats which bring about the general emergency reactions.*

(5) *Certain other basic problems have not been dealt with because of limitations of space.* Among these are (a) the problem of values in any definitive motivation theory, (b) the relation between appetites, desires, needs and what is "good" for the organism, (c) the

14

etiology of the basic needs and their possible derivation in early childhood, (d) redefinition of motivational concepts, i.e., drive, desire, wish, need, goal, (e) implication of our theory for hedonistic theory, (f) the nature of the uncompleted act, or success and failure, and of aspiration-level, (g) the role of association, habit and conditioning, (h) relation to the theory of inter-personal relations, (i) implications for psychotherapy, (j) implication for theory of society, (k) the theory of selfishness, (l) the relation between needs and cultural patterns, (m) the relation between this theory and Allport's theory of functional autonomy. These as well as certain other less important questions must be considered as motivation theory attempts to become definitive.

NOTES

1. Maslow, A. H. A preface to motivation theory. *Psychosomatic Med.*, 1943, 5, 85-92.

2. Wertheimer, M. Unpublished lectures at the New School for Social Research.

3. Goldstein, K. *The organism.* New York: American Book Co., 1939.

4. Freud, S. *New introductory lectures on psychoanalysis.* New York: Norton, 1933.

5. Adler, A. *Social interest.* London: Faber & Faber, 1938.

6. Cannon, W. B. *Wisdom of the body.* New York: Norton, 1932.

7. Young, P. T. The experimental analysis of appetite. *Psychol. Bull.*, 1941, 38, 129-164.

8. Maslow, A preface to motivation theory, *op cit.*

9. As the child grows up, sheer knowledge and familiarity as well as better motor development make these "dangers" less and less dangerous and more and more manageable. Throughout life it may be said that one of the main conative functions of education is this neutralizing of apparent dangers through knowledge, e.g., I am not afraid of thunder because I know something about it.

10. Shirley, M. Children's adjustments to a strange situation. *J. abnorm. (soc.) Psychol.*, 1942, 37, 201-217.

11. A "test battery" for safety might be confronting the child with a small exploding firecracker, or with a bewhiskered face, having the mother leave the room, putting him upon a high ladder, a hypodermic injection, having a mouse crawl up to him, etc. Of course I cannot seriously recommend the deliberate use of such "tests" for they might very well harm the child being tested. But these and similar situations come up by the score in the child's ordinary day-to-day living and may be observed. There is no reason why these stimuli should not be used with, for example, young chimpanzees.

12. Not all neurotic individuals feel unsafe. Neurosis may have at its core a thwarting of the affection and esteem needs in a person who is generally safe.

13. Maslow, A. H., & Mittelmann, B. *Principles of abnormal psychology.* New York: Harper & Bros., 1941.

14. Goldstein, *op cit.*

15. Maslow & Mittelmann, *op cit.*

16. For further details see Maslow, A. H. The dynamics of psychological security-insecurity. *Character & Pers.*, 1942, 10, 331-344 and Plant, J. *Personality and the cultural pattern.* New York: Commonwealth Fund, 1937, Chapter 5.

17. Whether or not this particular desire is universal we do not know. The crucial question, especially important today, is "Will men who are enslaved and dominated, inevitably feel dissatisfied and rebellious?" We may assume on the basis of commonly known clinical data that a man who has known true freedom (not paid for by giving up safety and security but rather built on the basis of adequate safety and security) will not willingly or easily allow his freedom to be taken away from him. But we do not know that this is true for the person born into slavery. The events of the next decade should give us our answer. See discussion of this problem in Fromm, E. *Escape from freedom.* New York: Farrar and Rinehart, 1941.

18. Perhaps the desire for prestige and respect from others is subsidiary to the desire for self-esteem or confidence in oneself. Observation of children seems to indicate that this is so, but clinical data give no clear support for such a conclusion.

19. Kardiner, A. *The traumatic neuroses of our time.* New York: Hoeber, 1941. For more extensive discussion of normal self-esteem, as well as for reports of various researchers, see Maslow, A. H., Dominance, personality and social behavior in women. *J. soc. Psychol.*, 1939, 10, 3-39.

20. Clearly creative behavior, like painting, is like any other behavior in having multiple determinants. It may be seen in "innately creative" people whether they are satisfied or not, happy or unhappy, hungry or sated. Also it is clear that creative activity may be compensatory, ameliorative or purely economic. It is my impression (as yet unconfirmed) that it is possible to distinguish the artistic and intellectual products of basically satisfied people from those of basically unsatisfied people by inspection alone. In any case, here too we must distinguish, in a dynamic fashion, the overt behavior itself from its various motivations or purposes.

21. Wertheimer, *op cit.*

22. Levy, D. M. Primary affect hunger. *Amer. J. Psychiat.*, 1937, 94, 643-652.

23. I am aware that many psychologists and psychoanalysts use the term "motivated" and "determined" synonymously, *e.g.*, Freud. But I consider this an obfuscating usage. Sharp distinctions are necessary for clarity of thought, and precision in experimentation.

24. To be discussed fully in a subsequent publication.

25. The interested reader is referred to the very excellent discussion of this point in Murray, H. A., *et al. Explorations in personality*. New York: Oxford University Press, 1938.

26. Tolman, E. C. *Purposive behavior in animals and men*. New York: Century, 1932.

27. Maslow, A. H. Conflict, frustration, and the theory of threat. *J. abnorm. (soc.) Psychol.*, 1943, 38, 81-86.

28. Note that acceptance of this theory necessitates basic revision of the Freudian theory.

29. If we were to use the word "sick" in this way, we should then also have to face squarely the relations of man to his society. One clear implication of our definition would be that (1) since a man is to be called sick who is basically thwarted, and (2) since such basic thwarting is made possible ultimately only by forces outside the individual, then (3) sickness in the individual must come ultimately from a sickness in the society. The "good" or healthy society would then be defined as one that permitted man's highest purposes to emerge by satisfying all his prepotent basic needs.

CPSIA information can be obtained at www.ICGtesting.com
Printed in the USA
BVOW02s0057130913

331037BV00002B/28/P

"Shannon has a wonderful ability to translate the truths of God's Word into interactive Bible studies that speak to relevant issues women face today. *Control Girl* is a penetrating look at how selfishness and self-protectiveness wreck lives—and why surrender and trust are God's life-giving pathways to true freedom and joy."

Nancy DeMoss Wolgemuth, author and Revive Our Hearts teacher and host

"Authentic, relevant, and truth-filled, *Control Girl* is written especially for any woman longing for security, peace, and joy. Through her Bible-based teaching and humorous stories, Shannon reminds us God never intends us to carry around the burden of control, and instead offers us the gift of sweet surrender to him. I finished *Control Girl* being reminded afresh that for those who love God, there awaits the happiest Happy Ending imaginable. Hooray! Highly recommended!"

Cindy Bultema, women's speaker, Bible teacher, and author of *Red Hot Faith*

"In the style of Liz Curtis Higgs, *Control Girl* is an easy and entertaining read, yet Shannon Popkin packs a punch where we so need it if we are to be set free from the stressful habit that robs our joy and ruins our relationships!"

Dee Brestin, author of *Idol Lies*

"No one wants to be enslaved to anger, anxiety, or fear. Yet many battle those emotions without making any headway in their struggle to fix themselves and others. In *Control Girl*, my longtime friend Shannon Popkin offers an alternative strategy. She shows how biblical thinking helps readers understand the conditions of their hearts so that they can find freedom in true spiritual growth through the wisdom of the Word and the power of the Holy Spirit. I highly recommend it."

Dr. Chris Brauns, pastor of The Red Brick Church and author of *Unpacking Forgiveness* and *Bound Together*

"When you start out reading a book for an endorsement and it becomes your Bible study, that is a good sign. Instead of making notes about how good the book is, I found myself writing down how God was using Shannon's words to address the heart of my own control issues. . . . *Control*

Girl is helping me solidify my foundation as a Jesus Girl, giving me confidence to practice surrender first and be OK with God not answering all my questions."

Jen Ferguson, coauthor of *Pure Eyes, Clean Heart: A Couple's Journey to Freedom from Pornography*

"If you've ever struggled with control issues, read this book. With personal vulnerability, biblical depth, powerful personal illustrations, and pointed application questions, Shannon Popkin reveals how seven women of the Bible can teach us how to surrender our will to God's design for our future.... It's ideal for personal use or for small-group studies."

Carol Kent, speaker and author of *Becoming a Woman of Influence*

"Psst . . . You there . . . the one with the control issues. I know you have a craving to control. We all do. We have since the garden of Eden, but there's hope! In this funny, tender, and truth-telling book, Shannon Popkin peels back the layers of our control problem. If that sounds a bit like a root canal, wait until you crack the cover. In a tone that feels like coffee with a close friend, Shannon bravely goes first, letting us see the reality of her own need to control while simultaneously pointing us to the hope found in God's Word. You will find your heart warming, your lips smiling, and your fists unclenching as Shannon leads you away from control and toward sweet surrender. A must-read for every woman east of the garden."

Erin Davis, author, blogger, and recovering Control Girl

"Shannon gets painfully honest and to the point as she challenges all of us Control Girls to surrender that burden and experience the Happy Ending God has planned! . . . She takes us through the lives of seven women from Scripture to help us discern more readily when we are grabbing for control rather than walking in the rest that Christ provides."

Kimberly Wagner, author of *Fierce Women: The Power of a Soft Warrior* and coauthor of *Men Who Love Fierce Women*

"Delightful. Insightful. Helpful. Popkin's sweet blend of storytelling and Scripture helps the medicine go down. If you're a control freak, this study is just what the doctor ordered."

Mary A. Kassian, author of *Girls Gone Wise*

control girl

Lessons *on* Surrendering Your Burden *of* Control *from* Seven Women *in the* Bible

SHANNON POPKIN

Kregel
Publications

ISBN 978-0-8254-4429-6

Printed in the United States of America
19 20 21 22 23 24 25 26 27 28 / 12 11 10 9 8 7 6

To Ken—
who inspires me to become
a Jesus Girl

Contents

Acknowledgments

❀ KEN: THANKS for loving me, leading me, and letting me share my message. You're the ink in my pen. Lindsay, Cole, and Cade: My sweet kids, I love you so. Thanks for having love that always hopes and always perseveres, even when I'm not at my best (but boys, you know it makes it worse when you sing the Control Girl song). May you always fly to Jesus with your every need. My parents: I'm so proud to claim you. Dad, you're the kind of father I wish every girl had. Mom, your gracious way of serving, giving, and loving inspires me to be a Jesus Girl.

Chris and Jamie Brauns: Your friendship is a gift. Chris, you may deserve credit for first discovering my inner Control Girl with a McDonald's cup in hand. Thanks for inspiring me to write and investing in me for so many years. Jamie, thanks for helping me sort out life while I sort laundry. This book, in large part, is a recap of our conversations. Jackie VanDyke: From the junior high bus to trails and treadmills, we're on this journey together. Your input, both on what the Bible says and how to live its message, is such a gift to me. Angela Gebhard: Thanks for loving me and my family. Your love for Jesus makes me want to love him more. My favorite visits with you are when we cry. Cindy Bultema: Your confetti-like encouragement is catching. Thanks for taking me under your wing and inspiring me to keep going. Del and Deb Fehsenfeld: God has blessed me so much with your encouragement and writing guidance over the years.

And to the "Prayeriors," you powerful women of prayer (plus a couple of men), my partners in the fight: Mom and Dad, Ken, Karen G., Aunt Jo, Jamie, Cindy, Jackie V., Angela, Renee, Ingrid, Michelle L., Darcie, Dawn, Deb S., Marie, Missy, Jessica, Deb F., Cheryl, Stacy, Lori, Mara, Nicole, Kristi, Beth, Brenda, Hilma, Sue, Wendi, Tabby, Brie, Lindsay, Hannah,

Sarah, Renell, Jackie S., Amy, Jocelyn, Michelle G., Ruth, Carrie, and Lisa—thank you! Your faithful prayers and encouragement have more than doubled my armor.

Jeff Manion, Dan Wright, and Marie Mossner: Thanks for your ministry to our church and for investing in me personally. Thanks to my agent, Karen Neumair, for seeing the potential and encouraging me every step of the twisty-turn way. I am so thankful for Credo and you. And I'm so honored to work with the wonderful people at Kregel Publications. Janyre: I'm blessed not only to have you edit my work but to have gained a dear friend in the process. Sarah, Micah, Katherine, and Noelle: I am so thankful for your keen insight and gracious help. In addition, I'm grateful for the input and guidance from my writer and speaker friends, Paula Marsteller, Erin Davis, Alice Daniels, Rachel Norton, Susie Finkbeiner, and Susan Tebos. Thanks to those who have shared their stories with me and participated in my forums. You know who you are.

And most of all, thanks to Jesus, whose love has washed me clean and whose Spirit lays down the arrows and compels me forward in joy. My hope is to please you.

Introduction
My "Happy" Ending

🌼 MY HUSBAND teased that it was only right to dedicate this book to him. "Without me," he said, "you'd still be going along in life thinking you were agreeable!"

He's right. Before I got married, I didn't realize I was a Control Girl, probably because I could control most everything in my little life. I would come home from teaching second grade every day and take a nap. At about six o'clock, I'd shuffle to the kitchen for a snack-ish dinner, and then get ready to go out. I was a youth leader, I attended Bible studies, I met friends for coffee. I liked being with people, and so I was . . . constantly.

Then I met Ken. When we started dating, I scheduled our weekends from top to bottom with social activities. But after a few months of this, my not-so-social boyfriend said he'd had enough.

Enough? I had never *heard* of enough socializing. I borrowed from sleep, savings, time with God—whatever it took—in order to be social. If there were people gathering, I wanted to be among them. And now I wanted Ken to be among them too. But that's not what he wanted.

He proposed a one-night-out-per-weekend compromise, which was my first taste of giving up control. But since I was still enamored and starry-eyed, it wasn't hard to deny myself and cheerfully spend more evenings in than out.

When we got married, it was harder. I could no longer take naps after school and still have dinner ready. And without my naps, I was too tired to stay out late with friends. Suddenly, I was losing control, and I didn't like it. Ken, who had once filled me with joy, now filled me with anger. I kept telling him, "I was always so carefree and cheerful before I met you."

One Friday night in early marriage, a young couple from down the street invited us over for dinner. I was almost giddy, sure that they were going to be our new best friends. Ken was less than giddy. Not only was he less social than I, he was also exhausted. Ken is a driven, self-motivated kind of guy who gets up at four thirty in the morning, leaving him little leftover energy for Friday nights.

After a lovely dinner with our neighbors, they led us to the living room. Our conversation progressed nicely, but I noticed Ken wasn't saying much. I glanced down to where he was sitting, petting the dog on the floor, and I noticed his hand, limp on the dog's back. His head was drooping at a strange angle. *Oh no*, I thought. *He's asleep!*

From where the neighbors were sitting, they couldn't see Ken's face, so I crossed my fingers and hoped they would think he was just oddly staring at their dog. I tried to hold their attention by talking faster and with more animation. But then someone asked Ken a question.

I nudged him with my foot, and his head yanked upward. He made some unintelligible remark with slightly slurred speech. I was mortified.

The neighbors laughed good-heartedly and said, "You must be exhausted." So this beautiful evening, with these people who were now *not* going to be our new best friends, came to a screeching halt. They showed us to the door, and we walked down the sidewalk toward home.

In that space of about five driveways, I packed a lot in. "Unbelievable! You humiliated me! From now on, mister, you are guzzling coffee before we go anywhere!" I spat the words into the darkness, pumping my arms with disgust. My husband lagged behind, saying nothing.

It's one of those ugly Control Girl moments I wish I could forget.

CAN I CONTROL MY HAPPY ENDING?

It wasn't until years later—after adding kids, dogs, a house, jobs, and responsibilities to our lives—that I realized I have control issues. Rather than being squelched under the chaos of family life, my control cravings have mushroomed.

Nowadays, I not only feel responsible for things like keeping my husband awake at dinner parties, I also have an urgent desire to keep my daughter's bangs from hanging in her eyes. And an absolute need to keep crumbs out of bedsheets. And an intense passion to keep socks from being stuffed under the couch, boots from being tracked on the carpeting, and noses from being picked in church. Not to mention the big things I'd like to control!

Now, I don't mean to be exasperating. I'm actually trying to make everything turn out right. I only control because I care so much. The more invested I am, the more I clamp down, on either the person I love or some outcome I can't live without. The things I'm trying to control in the moment are almost always linked to the Happy Ending I've got all worked out in my head.

While it may seem like I'm obsessing over the superficial, my heart projects much further and deeper. *What if he gets teased for nose-picking?* I worry. *What if she never learns to be responsible? Where will this all lead?* When I take control, I'm just trying to clear obstacles and make straight the path to my Happy Ending.

But here's the irony. Though I've lunged for control in hundreds of ways and instances, I've never been able to safeguard my life from heartache. And by taking control, I've actually created anguish for the people I love, rather than protecting them from it. By trying to control everything, I've created strife and misery for everyone—including me. Without meaning to, I've sabotaged my own Happy Ending.

Can you relate? Do you push for your own version of a Happy Ending? Do you project out into the future, then take control because you're convinced that it's up to you to make things turn out right? If so, what has the outcome been? Have you been able to lock down any air-tight Happy Endings yet?

Me neither.

Here's what I'm coming to realize: the Happy Ending in my head is an illusion. It's impossible, because in order to pull it off, I would have to live a life of white-knuckled misery, trying to control everything and keep it all on track. This would make for quite an Unhappy Ending, not to mention all of the unhappy moments in between.

CONTROL GIRLS IN THE BIBLE

My interest in Control Girls in the Bible started with Eve. I was painting the laundry room and listening to John Piper preach a sermon on the curse in Genesis 3 and how Eve's "desire to rule over her husband" was actually a desire for control.[1] With paintbrush in hand, it occurred to me that I, a daughter of Eve, was also cursed with a desire for control.

Later, I combed through Scripture, curious to uncover any control issues in other daughters of Eve. Turns out, it's hard to find women in the Bible who *weren't* Control Girls. As I studied, I found that Eve, Sarah, Hagar, Rebekah, Leah, Rachel, and Miriam each struggled with control the way I do. They took matters into their own hands, tried to make everything turn out right, and made everybody miserable in the process.

Some of the most famous scenes in the Bible hinge on Control Girls who were trying to contend for their own preferences. The Bible, you'll recall, is a story all about God and his people. And yet, these women were making it all about *them*. The nerve, right? But this is my struggle too. I hijack the story God's still writing, ignore his greater purposes, and make the story all about me and my Happy Ending. Is there a way to keep from repeating history?

I invite you to join me on a study of these interesting Control Girls from the past. We'll climb the wall dividing our lives from theirs and lower ourselves into their ancient stories. We'll mine each one, looking for warnings and lessons for ourselves and new insights about God.

I've divided each chapter into lessons with a correlating Bible passage to read first. Please, oh please, don't skip these Bible readings! I wouldn't want you to miss out on the power that God's Word can unleash when you hear from him directly. You'll notice that some chapters have more lessons than others. That's because I want to let the women of the Bible lead our discussion, and some have more to say than others. And you'll find the shorter chapters a nice break. Each lesson has questions at the end that will help you make the content personal. I hope you'll use a notebook to journal your thoughts, reactions, and plans. If you're studying as a group, leaders are welcome to download a free discussion guide at ShannonPopkin.com.

As we study together, I think you'll find one consistent theme: surrender. The only way any Control Girl of the Bible ever found the security, peace, and joy she was longing for was when she did the opposite of taking control—when she surrendered to God and made her story all about him. It's the same for us today.

God never intended for us to carry around the burden of trying to control everything. He designed us to live in sweet surrender to him, trusting him with all that seems to threaten our future happiness. For those who love God, there awaits an ultimate Happy Ending. And if the end of the story is secure, we can flip back to any unsettling circumstance of the present and forfeit the burden of having to take control.

Surrender to God is what guards us against lives of white-knuckled misery. Rather than lunging after control, Jesus invites us to say as he did, "Not my will, but yours, be done" (Luke 22:42). Jesus invites us to follow him on a path of surrender to a place where God is in control and we are free. That's where I want to go. Who's coming with me?

Chapter One
Path of a Control Girl

✿ WHEN MY daughter was six, we moved into a new house. She insisted on having the small bedroom looking out over the driveway, rather than the larger one facing the pretty, wooded back yard. When I asked why, she said she wanted to be sure to see the garbage trucks when they came to pick up our trash. Years later, she asked why her brother got the "good room" facing the back yard. I chuckled and said, "Don't you remember, honey? You wanted to see the garbage trucks!"

In life, we make a lot of choices and decisions based on what we're hoping for. We take one path and not another because of some goal we have in mind. But often we're like a six-year-old enamored with garbage trucks. Our perspective is skewed, and our goals are underdeveloped.

What if there were Someone who could see up ahead who knew beforehand what was going to make us happy in the long run? What if he could be in charge of what path we took and where it all led?

Actually, there is Someone. His name is God.

If we ignore God and take our own path, we'll inevitably end up at a trash pile that has lost its appeal. But if we follow God and trust his eternal perspective, he'll lead us—eventually—to a room with a more fabulous view than our six-year-old minds could even fathom.

Lesson 1: A Rutted-Out Path
Read Proverbs 3:1–12

I HAVE A gray video game controller in my basement that looks just like the other controllers, but it's not. It doesn't work.

I bought it at a garage sale and would have thrown it out, except that it solved a really big problem in our home. Our youngest son was two at the time, and whenever the older kids played video games, he would climb all over them—tugging, biting, scratching—doing whatever he could to pry the controllers from their hands. But the gray controller eliminated the problem. The big kids would settle him into a beanbag chair, place it in his chubby hands, and say, "There you go, buddy. There's *your* controller."

He was completely satisfied. He would jam his thumbs on the buttons, convinced that he was moving the little men on the screen. He was oblivious to the fact that not only was his controller broken, it wasn't even plugged in.

Even though I don't play video games, I'm a lot like my boy, Cade. My gaze is locked on the scenes playing out on the big screen of life—especially the ones that involve people I love—and it feels like I'm in control. I might not be pushing actual buttons, but I do have a strong sense that I am shaping the future. In fact, I feel *responsible* for making everything turn out right. Our Happy Ending rests in my hands.

This is why I call myself a Control Girl. I *think* I'm in control.

Now I wouldn't *say* I'm in control. I would say that God is. I've read the Bible. I know the stories of the flood, Lot's wife turning to salt, and the parting of the Red Sea. If you pointed to a story in the Bible and said, "See? God is in control," I would nod my head in agreement. Yes, I believe this. Completely.

But then, what do I do when my teen begins dating someone I disapprove of? Or my coworker is withholding information and making decisions without me? Or my husband shrugs off my concerns about the musty smell in the basement? With an eye on the future and where this all might lead, I suddenly morph into . . . Control Girl. My voice gets louder and more intense. I become manipulative or direct. Like a kid who just lost a round on his video game, I lean forward with greater intensity and determination, convinced that it's all up to me to set things straight.

In these instances, my demeanor necessarily raises the question: **Do I *truly* believe that God is in control? Or do I secretly think I am?**

Also, what is God's reaction? Does he shrug off my insistence that it's all up to me? It's one thing to let a toddler carry on with a façade. But what if *I'm* the one clutching my illusion of control with sweaty, frantic hands? Does God just wag his head in disbelief and let me continue in my panicky frustration and angst?

No. Out of kindness, God leans down to dangle the cord of my teeny-weeny controller before me. Gently, he says, "See? Honey, you're not plugged in." God wants to free me of this control-burden, which was never mine to carry in the first place. *God* is in control; not me. He invites me to live like I believe this.

That's what these cord-dangling moments are: invitations.

Sometimes God uses something drastic—like a car crash, ongoing infertility, or a tornado—to expose my lack of control. But other times, he tucks his invitation into something smaller. Like a certain towel I encountered on the bathroom floor.

MY HEART'S RUT

One morning, I gave my middle schooler a crash course in bathroom etiquette. He had recently begun showering in our guest bathroom, and I didn't want guests tripping over damp towels and yesterday's jeans.

My training was thorough. After cheerfully giving clear instructions, I also required several walk-throughs that included hanging up a towel and throwing clothes in the hamper. I felt good about my constructive approach and was confident the bathroom would now be guest-ready at any moment.

But that evening, after everyone was in bed, I walked into the bathroom and stopped short. There were my son's sweaty soccer clothes and damp towel in a familiar little heap on the bathroom floor. I couldn't believe it. I stood over the defiant pile with my fists clenched and my jaw tightened, contemplating my next steps.

There is a certain path, deeply rutted in my heart. I've repented of this path many times, yet in that moment it seemed like the right way to go. It beckoned to me with logic, clear and strong, whispering, "He doesn't listen to you. He doesn't follow your instructions. What's going to happen to him if you do nothing? He's going to fail. You've got to do something! You've got to do something right *now*."

And so I set off down the path of the Control Girl.

Filling my lungs with air, I bellowed my son's name. I yelled it again and again until he appeared, blinking groggily, from his bedroom. I jabbed my finger in the direction of the sweaty heap. He hung his head, and I began bludgeoning him with my words. Repeatedly I pounded his dignity with my narrowed eyes and sneering attacks. I didn't touch him, but his expression told me that my words had squeezed his heart.

As I snarled, I dismissed several fleeting thoughts that I might regret this later. It felt *good* to berate him. He needed to learn to follow instructions. What sort of student or employee would he become if he didn't listen?

The sense of power was intoxicating, and I wanted more. I felt myself gaining control. Yes, I was making things right. I was in control. Now the world was a better place because I was ruling over the stinky piles of laundry littering my son's life. I would rule over my family's towels, and all would be good and right and peaceful.

But thirty minutes later nothing felt good. Nothing felt right. And nothing felt peaceful. My heart had deceived me. Once again, I had taken the path of the Control Girl.

I knelt at my son's bedside with tears of agonizing regret. Though he accepted my apology, I couldn't retract what I had said. I couldn't erase the look that had flickered across his face as my critical words cut in. I had followed my craving for control, and oh, what an ugly place it led me to.

Getting My Hooks In

It's hard for me to replay that for you. I generally like to keep my inner Control Girl well-cloaked. My tactical control moves are usually behind-closed-doors operations.

So why am I ushering you into this ugly scene from my bathroom? I do so because, while the whole world is peacefully sleeping, perhaps I'm not the only Control Girl still up, obsessing about my child's future or erupting over a towel.

Knowing how carefully I hide my own agenda, I figure there might be other secret Control Girl operations going on too. Maybe you and I have more in common than we'd like to admit. But even if you'd prefer to remain a closet Control Girl rather than going public the way I have, there's something you should know. Somebody leaked our secret to the press, quite awhile ago.

Way back in Genesis 3, after the first woman lost the very first battle for control, God made it public. He told Eve that she would be cursed with an insatiable desire to take control—to force the things that look so good and right in *her* eyes (whether fruit from a tree or a wet towel on the floor) into the hands of her loved ones. She would not only crave control, she would be convinced that she *should* take control. Eve and all of her daughters would be Control Girls.

How many times have I lived out Eve's curse, believing that it was good and right to take control? The towel incident is only one of many scars on my memory from times I've gotten my hooks in and hurt the people I love.

What an ugly, diminished version of myself I become when I try to take control into my own hands! But sometimes God's hands seem so far away. His throne seems to sit so far above where I stand, reigning over the little heap on the floor. Can God really be trusted with my Happy Ending? Does he even care about the things that concern me?

He can, and he does. In fact, it's *because* God cares that he leans down to dangle the cord of my teeny-weeny controller before me.

Out of kindness, God exposes my lack of control and personally invites me to trust him—with the towel lying at my feet, with the end of the story, and with everything in between.

Proverbs 3:5–6 says,

> Trust in the LORD with all your heart,
> and do not lean on your own understanding.

> In all your ways acknowledge him,
>> and he will make straight your paths.

This passage points me in the opposite direction of my Control Girl path. Rather than letting me lunge for control based on my limited perspective, God invites me to look up, surrender to him, and relish the fact that he's in control and I am not.

Friends, let's take a different path, shall we? Let's unclamp our sweaty hands from that illusion of control we've been gripping. Let's lay that broken, unplugged controller in the hands of the one who truly is in control: God.

* Take inventory of your life. Are you living as though *you're* in control or as though God is? What indications do you see?

* Read Proverbs 3:5–6 again, and list any contrast you see between these verses and the path of the Control Girl. Pray these verses over a situation you're tempted to control.

* List any cord-dangling moments God has used to expose your lack of control. Read Proverbs 3:11–12, and write "Proof that God loves me" above your list.

For Meditation: Proverbs 3:5–6

Rather than letting me continue in my illusion of control, God kindly exposes my lack of control and invites me to trust him instead. *God, thank you for reminding me that you are in control so I don't have to be.*

Lesson 2: Beneath Anger and Anxiety
Read Jeremiah 17:5–10

ONE SUMMER, WHEN my boys were little, they complained about bees in the basement. They'd holler, "Mommy, there's another bee flying around down here!" But rather than going down to check it out, I kept calling back, "OK, just leave it alone."

Did I think these bees would just find their way back outside? I'm not sure. I guess it was easiest to just ignore the problem and hope it went away.

Then the boys complained about dead bees near the window. Again, I kept saying, "OK, just leave them alone." I promised to clean the bees up once I was down there. The trouble was, I hardly ever went down to the basement. It was the kids' playroom, and they had complete jurisdiction. Weeks went by without me setting foot in the area of the reported bees.

Then one day, little Cole came upstairs and looked me in the eye. He said, "Mom, this bee thing is creeping me out. I think I hear bees buzzing in the wall."

"What?" I said, jumping up with instant alarm. "Show me!"

I was astounded at what I found. There were *hundreds* of bees lying dead along the windowsills. And Cole was right. There was definitely a buzzing sound in the wall—right next to where my boys were playing.

Within hours, a bee expert was telling me, "You called just in time. If those bees had burrowed through your drywall—" I didn't let him finish the sentence. I didn't want us all to have nightmares.

MY HEART'S BASEMENT

Friends, our controlling natures are like a nest of bees burrowing through our hearts. The trouble is, we hardly ever make it down to the heart level. It's easier to ignore the warnings and pretend no problem exists. But just as the bees in my basement were never going to magically see themselves out, so it is with our basement-level control issues. It's dangerous to let the problem stay hidden, especially from ourselves.

So look yourself in the eye. Take a trip to your heart's basement. Do you hear any buzzing? Could there be a Control Girl lurking in your heart? If so, it's time to stop ignoring the warnings and confront the issue.

ANGER

For many years, I thought my problem was anger. And clearly, as I demonstrated in lesson 1, I did (and do) struggle with anger. But even after reading books on anger, praying about it for years, and having friends hold me accountable, I couldn't be free of it.

I had a vague sense that there was some deeper problem causing me to erupt over something as silly as a towel on the bathroom floor, but I rarely went down to the basement of my heart to examine the problem. Then one day, I heard Dee Brestin talking on the radio about the "sin beneath the sin." Dee said that we often fail to conquer a besetting sin because we attack the surface sin instead of the deeper, root sin.[1]

At this point in my life, God had just begun to show me the ugliness of my control problem. For the first time, I realized that anger was my surface sin, and the "sin beneath the sin" was my desire for control. Not until I began linking these two—anger and control—did I get some traction with managing my anger.

Anger is easy for me to spot in myself. I know when I'm angry and when my anger is wrong. But it's much harder for me to see my heart's sinful bent on control. Jeremiah 17:9 says, "The heart is deceitful above all things, and desperately sick; who can understand it?"

For me to know my heart, I need regular trips to the "basement." So when I feel anger rising, I've learned to probe deeper and ask, "OK, Shannon. What are you trying to control?" For me, dealing only with my anger, and never the deeper issue of control, was like sweeping up a few bees and ignoring the burrowed-in hive.

Maybe you can relate to my ongoing anger struggle. Perhaps you have towel stories of your own. If so, as you work through this book, start keeping a journal of angry outbursts, and consider whether these indicate a deeper struggle with control. When you feel anger rising, ask yourself:

What am I trying to control?
Am I angry because I've lost control of someone or something?

Look for connections and record them.

ANXIETY

Perhaps you are someone who never gets angry. Maybe you would *never* raise your voice or throw a fit over a discarded towel. You don't struggle with anger; it's just not something you do.

Oh, how I've wished I could be like you. You seem so sweet and calm and perfect. But my friends who *are* like you—the ones who rarely get angry—tell me that they often struggle with something equally difficult: *anxiety*.

Instead of yelling and ranting behind closed doors, they're pacing and fretting. Or they're obsessing about germ-free kitchens and safety locks. In the same way that I lose control of my anger, they lose control of their fear. But the deeper "sin beneath the sin" causing the rise of anxiety is the same: control.

The day I spoke for Laura's moms group was the first day she had ever placed her ten-month-old in the church's childcare. She had never left him with anyone but her husband or mom, and when she sat down at the beginning of the meeting, she literally felt panic rising within her.

She wanted to spring from her chair, bolt to the nursery, and snatch him back into the safety of her arms. But something held her back. She had a gentle sense that the Lord wanted her to hear something that day. And that's when I got up to speak on control.

As I split open my private world and shared several incriminating Control Girl tales, Laura laughed nervously, secretly identifying. She had just endured the isolation of moving to a new town, a complicated pregnancy and birthing experience, and a rough recovery. In addition, her baby suffered from a litany of allergies plus feeding and sleep issues.

Like me, Laura had never linked her anxiety to an underlying struggle for control. She realized that she too was a Control Girl. Laura wrote me months later to say that although her situation hadn't changed, *she* had. By identifying and working through her deeper struggles with control, she had begun to have victory over anxiety.

Can you relate to Laura? Do you struggle with excessive fear or worry? Perhaps you would never lose your temper, but you could lose a night's sleep worried that your name might be on the short list for potential layoffs. Or you could lose your appetite fretting that your husband's plane might fall from the sky. Or you could lose touch with reality wondering if your teenager is unconscious in his crashed car because he is ten minutes late.

If you struggle with anxiety, begin keeping a journal of any excessive worry or obsessive fear, and consider whether you see indications of a deeper struggle with control. When you feel your anxiety rising, ask yourself:

> What do I crave having control over?
> What do I fear losing control of?

Look for connections and record them.

HOLD AND FOLD

In his parenting book, *Losing Control and Liking It*, Dr. Tim Sanford divides all of life into two categories: (1) what I can control, and (2) what I can't control. Ultimately, the only thing that fits into this first category is me. I can control my own actions, attitudes, and responses. Everything else goes into the second category.

Dr. Sanford suggests two responses: Hold and Fold. For category one, we should Hold control of ourselves. Picture your cupped hands, holding responsibility for yourself. Self-control is a fruit of the Spirit. We are being godly when we control ourselves. But for category two, we must Fold. Picture hands folded in prayer, giving God control of the things we can't. This also is a godly response.[2]

Control Girls do exactly the opposite of Hold and Fold. Consider my towel example once more. Can I ultimately control what my son does with his towel? No. I can use my influence to parent my son well, but I cannot control whether he becomes a responsible adult. This towel at my feet was an opportunity to Fold my hands and put God in charge of my (and my son's) Happy Ending. But instead of Folding, I grabbed. I took matters into my own Control Girl hands.

And what about Holding? Could I have controlled my own worry and anger in response to the towel? Yes, I could have, but I didn't. I tossed self-control aside and went on an angry, destructive rampage.

This is the great Control Girl irony.

As we try to control things we *can't* control, we tend to lose control of the one thing we can—ourselves. God invites us to reverse the process, to Hold and Fold.

Take some time to visit the basement of your heart. Here are some prompts to help you:

- ❀ Read Jeremiah 17:9–10. Ask God to help you see your heart clearly.

- ❀ Which surface-level sins are common for you? Anxiety? Anger? Both? Begin your journal by recording any recent episodes, along with any correlating struggles with control.

- ❀ Read Psalm 37:1–9 and record anything you find about anger, anxiety, or trusting God with your Happy Ending.

For Meditation: Psalm 37:8–9

My anger and anxiety often indicate a deeper heart-level struggle with control. *Lord, help me to Hold responsibility for myself and, with the things I can't control, help me to Fold my hands in surrender to you.*

Lesson 3: Where Am I Headed?
Read Romans 12:1–2

ONE MORNING IN Bible study, I asked the ladies in my group to share a prayer request concerning a relational struggle. I figured we might hear requests about rebellious teens or brittle marriages. Instead, each and every woman shared about the hurt and stress created by her overly controlling mom or mother-in-law.

I was stunned.

Now, granted, the holiday season was upon us. And like no other time of year, heightened holiday expectations bring out the control in the girl. But regardless of the calendar page, I was grieved by the raw pain these women, huddled around the table, were experiencing because of a controlling older woman in each of their lives.

I was also alarmed. In the weeks and months prior to this day, God had been showing me my own ravenous appetite for control. Clearly, these older Control Girls—a little further down the path than I—had not aged well. Would my own burning desire for control cause *me* to one day be the one stressing out my loved ones and making everyone miserable?

Surely these older women—the moms and moms-in-law who were the focus of my group's prayer requests that day—hadn't set out to exasperate their families. No bride walks down the aisle and says to her beloved, "One day, I will drive you nuts with my manipulative tactics." No new mother kisses the soft head of her newborn and says, "Someday, I will exasperate you with my endless criticisms and demands." Control is a problem that seems to metastasize, undetected, over time.

Had the process already begun in me? Solemnly, after all the prayer requests had been shared, I leaned in and said to my group, "I want us to support each other by praying about these difficult women in our lives. But, I'm just sitting here wondering . . . how do we not *become* them? How do we ensure that twenty years from now, it won't be *our* daughters and *our* daughters-in-law sharing prayer requests about *us?*" We looked at each other around the circle, and I could tell we didn't have answers. That haunting question is ultimately what prompted me to write this book.

Look around you. Perhaps you'll find, as I have, that controlling, older women are not in short supply. It's hard to find someone who *doesn't* have a controlling mom or mother-in-law. Oh, how I want my life to head in a different direction. Don't you?

A New Path

I wish that I could tell you that my Bible study epiphany cured me, that I looked myself in the eye and said, "See where this leads? You've got to stop trying to control everything." And then I stopped. But change requires more than just recognizing a problem or its consequences. Some mornings, I wake up with agonizing Control Girl regret, then I trip back into the same rutted-out behavior before even making it to breakfast.

The Bible not only instructs us to stop our sinful habits, but also says we must start doing the opposite, correct things (Col. 3:5–10). So, to curb greediness, we practice generosity. To reverse selfishness, we practice putting others first. And to overturn a pattern of control, we practice surrender.

Surrender is counterintuitive to a Control Girl. We have a natural posture of holding on to control rather than releasing it to God. **In order to reverse our natural bent, we have to cultivate a new demeanor toward God: surrender.**

Our mental image of surrender is often characterized by passivity. We talk about letting go. Giving God control. We picture lifting our hands in church as we softly sing along with the worship leader. Surrender seems so sweet and serene, under dimmed lights and air-conditioning vents.

But to say, as Jesus did, "Not my will, but yours, be done," is anything but passive and serene. It's active and gritty. Surrender might begin with hands lifted in worship, but it will culminate in the uphill challenge of relinquishing control. That's what surrender is.

Only a few steps in, our burning lungs and pounding hearts will scream for us to turn back downhill. We'll want to cave in to our weak-hearted Control Girl ways. So what will keep our feet to the path? What will fuel our uphill change? A new mind-set.

Thoughts are powerful. What we believe shapes the direction we take in life. So to change direction, we must change our thought patterns. Romans 12:2 says that transformation comes from renewing our minds. Colossians 3:10 says that we change by renewing what we know about God. So by hitting *refresh* on what we know about God, we can curb our controlling behavior.

It works like this: If I'm suspicious of God's motives, or I question whether he cares, I won't surrender to him. I'll trust in myself instead, and resort to Control Girl tactics. But what if I've just reminded myself that God not only is enthroned above the universe but also cares about me and is working all things together for my good? Well, then I've readied my heart to say, "Not my will, but yours, be done."

MEDITATING

Recently I sat at a coffee shop across the table from a young wife and mom who told me, "I actually have a lot of faith in God. I believe that he's in control and that I can trust him. But then, I try to control everything. Why is that? It doesn't make sense." I share my friend's conundrum.

How can we bridge the gap between what we say about God (that he's in control, and we trust him) and how we live (as if we're in control, and we trust ourselves)? We build this bridge, thought by thought, in our minds. The Bible calls it meditation.[3] Rather than emptying our minds, as Buddhists do, we fill our minds with the truth.

Meditation isn't necessarily learning something new, nor is it mindless, rote review. Meditation is pondering deeply and looking with fresh eyes at what we believe is truth. It's soaking our hearts in the significance of a particular truth by considering various angles and savoring the implications.

We act the way we act because we think the way we think. We take control because we think we must. Or perhaps we think no one will manage quite as well. Yet God already is in control. That's the truth, and if our behavior is ever to correspond, we must revamp the way we think. Do we want to stop being Control Girls? Transformation begins in our thought patterns. I'm so convinced of this that I've included a "meditation" for each lesson in this book. Each meditation encapsulates the lesson's main truth and provides a correlating Scripture passage.

Meditating on truth about God helps us cultivate this new mind-set of surrender. To meditate, you don't have to hum or sit in a certain position. Just take five minutes to read the truths. Read slowly. Think carefully about what they mean. Say them out loud, or pray them to God. Copy meaningful phrases or verses onto notecards to carry with you. Review them the next morning or evening.

When you reflect on truth, you wear new grooves in your mind. Then, when you encounter something you'd ordinarily want to control, your heart more readily flies to the truth. Rather than reacting with spikes of anger or anxiety (that send you stumbling into old ruts), you are postured for surrender. You're ready, and that is half the battle.

Here's my prediction. If I give full vent to my craving for control, it will turn me into someone I don't want to become. If I let my controlling heart lead me where it will, I'm convinced that someday, a woman in Bible study will ask for prayer about her exasperating mom or mother-in-law who's making everyone miserable, and it will be *me*. But if I start now and don't give up, if I cultivate a mind-set of surrender, and make a habit of saying, "Not my will, but yours, be done," transformation is possible. I can be changed from a Control Girl into a Jesus Girl.

- ✸ Take inventory of the older women in your life. Who has a demeanor of quiet surrender to God?

- ✸ How will you use the meditations provided for each lesson? Write out a detailed plan.

- ✸ Read Psalm 119:15–16. What difference does it make to go into a situation you'd like to control with a mind-set of surrender to God?

For Meditation: Romans 12:2

I am naturally bent on control, so surrender is counterintuitive. *God, I will cultivate a new mind-set of surrender by meditating on truth about you.*

Start with the Ending

WHEN I PUT God in charge of my Happy Ending, I concede what is true. He's in control, and I am not.

I do have choices, but every contingency in my life is attached to an ending held firmly in God's grasp. I'm not sure how this all works, but because God is kind and wise, this is good news. He is weaving together an ending far happier than anything I could construct.

If the ending *were* in my hands, I'd be in constant hysterics, trying to manage loose threads and snags. I'd surely be a frantic, obsessive Control Girl. But knowing that the last page of my story is settled gives me peace, security, and hope for the journey. If I start with the secure ending then flip backward, it's easier to give God control of the things that concern me *today*.

Even when my happiness seems to be unraveling, I am not undone, because I know that nothing has slipped from God's hands. In all things, I can say with confidence, "Not my will, but yours, be done."

Chapter Two
Eve: It Looked Good to Me

🌼 EVE'S STORY reads like a fairy tale in reverse. It begins with "happily ever after" and ends with the damsel in distress. Eve experienced what we'll never have—a perfect environment and a perfect relationship. Every sunrise pulled the curtain back on another day of exploring her surroundings and relationships.

But in true fairy-tale fashion, Eve was blissfully unaware of the heinous evil from which she had been shielded. One forbidden bite, and the page flipped forward to the "unhappily after" part of the story.

Lesson 1: Like Looking at an Eclipse
Read Genesis 3:1–7

DON'T YOU THINK it's interesting that God put the forbidden tree in the middle of the garden? When I don't want my kids to have something, I rarely place it in the *middle* of the table or the room. I tuck it away, out of sight.

But God planted the tree right in the center, perhaps where all of the garden paths converged. And he didn't hang the fruit ten feet up, covered in prickles, either. He let it dangle beautifully in the sunlight.

Why? Why did God make something *that* deadly so available and inviting?

For Adam and Eve, the tree posed a question: Would they trust God? As they brushed past the plump, juicy fruit on a daily basis, would they let God be in control? Would they live in sweet surrender to him? The fruit would serve as tangible evidence of their choice. Undisturbed, it signaled that God had control, over both the garden and them. It meant that all was well.

One day, when my son Cole was three, he wandered off. When I found him out in front of our house, I delivered a stern warning, explaining that there are bad people who drive through neighborhoods looking for little boys to steal. I warned that even if someone offered him candy, he must always stay away from strangers.

Cole listened with big, serious eyes, and then I tested him. I said, "Suppose a man pulls up and says, 'If you get in my car, I'll give you candy.' What will you say?"

Cole thought for a moment, and then answered earnestly, "Well . . . I would say . . . 'Can I have the whole bag?'"

It's humorous now. But back then, I was stunned by how little control I had over Cole's perspective. At three years old, he couldn't conceive of candy being offered by bad guys.

Similarly, Eve couldn't conceive of Satan's evil intentions. To her, Satan seemed almost neighborly when he asked, "Did God really say you can't eat *any* of this fruit?" Like a kidnapper asking, "Did your mom really say you can't *ever* eat candy?" Satan's exaggeration was a disdain-ful attack on God's character. He was subtly suggesting that perhaps God had control issues.

This is almost comical when you consider that God issued only one rule in the garden of Eden. Only *one*.

Why weren't there more? Why didn't God engrave his command-ments onto the trees, or pass out copies of Leviticus at orientation? It's because none of those rules were necessary. Good *looked* good to Adam and Eve. They naturally wanted good, and only good.

Just like nobody has to tell me not to eat mayonnaise by the spoon-ful, nobody had to tell Adam and Eve not to steal, lie, or kill. They natu-rally abhorred evil. They had no desire for it—at least, not as long as they abstained from the forbidden fruit.

It's ironic that Eve broke the rule, in part, because she wanted to see something. Satan said that this fruit would open her eyes. So what did she see immediately after eating the fruit?

"Then the eyes of both were opened, and they knew that they were naked" (Gen. 3:7).

OPENED EYES

Once, my friend's little boy was looking for her, but his daddy said, "Mommy's in the bathroom, changing. You can't go in there."

"Why not?" asked the boy.

The dad explained that Mommy wasn't dressed. "You can't see a naked woman. Not until you're married."

"So, after I get married," the boy said, "then I can see Mommy when she's naked?"

The humor in the story is that the boy couldn't care less whether his mom (or anybody, for that matter) was clothed or naked. His eyes weren't yet opened to nakedness—either the good *or* the evil related to nakedness. When he's older, no one will have to explain why watching his mom get dressed would be evil. Nor will anyone have to explain why helping his bride unbutton her wedding dress will be *good*. His eyes will be opened to the difference between good and evil.

This distinction between good and evil, however, is kept safe only when it is kept from us. God intended to be the keeper of this distinction forever. So he tucked the knowledge of good and evil into leafy branches of a tree, and guarded it with his one and only rule.

When Eve bit into that fruit, yes, her eyes were opened. She suddenly saw something she hadn't, but her eyes weren't designed to see it. It was like looking into a solar eclipse. Her eyesight was ruined.

With her feminine little hand, Eve ushered mankind into the era the Bible describes as "this present darkness" (Eph. 6:12). Evil began to look good to us, and good looked evil. The distinctions between the two became warped by our darkened understanding (Eph. 4:18).

New Rules

By breaking God's one and only rule, Adam and Eve made new rules necessary. Hundreds of them. God provided his Law (including the Ten Commandments) as a corrective lens, to help us see good and evil the way he does.

However, the Law can't *fix* our eyesight. It merely points out how dim our perspective is and how evil our hearts have become. The Law shows us our need for Jesus, the Light of the World. Jesus came that we might turn from darkness to light (Acts 26:18). Turning to Jesus is the exact reversal of Eve's story in the garden. When we follow Eve's example, we become Control Girls; when we follow Jesus's example and say as he did, "Not my will, but yours, be done" (Luke 22:42), we become Jesus Girls. Just like Eve, we have a choice: Control Girl or Jesus Girl.

- A Control Girl detaches from God. A Jesus Girl relies on him.
- A Control Girl breaks God's rules. A Jesus Girl embraces the Bible's instructions.
- A Control Girl trusts her own perspective. A Jesus Girl defers to God's viewpoint.

Control Girls don't like restrictions. They want to be in control and decide for themselves what is right and wrong. But women who are sweetly surrendered to God let him decide. They live day by day brushing up against all sorts of appealing—but destructive—options. Rather than reaching for the forbidden things, they trust God when he says something is harmful.

Control Girls and Jesus Girls are set apart by their perspectives on right and wrong. Who gets to decide? A Control Girl trusts her own viewpoint; a Jesus Girl defers to God's. She believes that God's restrictions lead to a lush, satisfying life, not a life of deprivation.

MY EYES OR GOD'S

I once expressed concern after a woman told me of her upcoming divorce. But she brushed my concern aside, explaining that divorce was what she and her husband wanted. She told me that months earlier, in a moment of honesty, her husband had confided that he was miserable in their marriage. This surprised her. She had been holding on for his sake. But now that she knew his true feelings, how could she hold him hostage? Instead, she was setting him free. Their divorce was almost final, and she was glowing with love for a new fiancé.

I walked away stunned. I had never heard such a sweet, warm, selfless description of divorce. The way this woman's life was falling into place seemed good and right to her. But would God call her divorce good? Or would he call it forbidden fruit, hanging tantalizingly in the sunlight?

At times, what God calls good (like staying in a difficult marriage) might not *seem* good to me. And like Eve in the garden, God asks me to choose his view over my own. Even before sin, God asked Eve to defer to his vantage point. He will ask no less of me today. God wants me to trust that his restrictions—first his tree rule and now his Bible full of commandments—will help me enjoy life the way he originally intended.

This isn't easy. Sometimes God's Word seems harsh and severe—especially when the culture at large has decided that God's ways are restrictive and narrow-minded. But when I'm tempted to chafe against God's perspective, it helps to picture the cross in the background. There, God sacrificed his Son for me. He loves me. He isn't barking out orders because he wants to make me miserable; he's inviting me out of the darkness. Will I turn from my dim perspective and come enjoy life the way my Creator intended?

- ❋ How does Isaiah 5:20–21 reflect Eve's story?

- ❋ Read Ephesians 4:17–24, and list the characteristics of someone with darkened understanding versus one who knows Jesus.

- ❋ Describe your spiritual eyesight. Are you trusting your own perspective over God's? How will you give control to God?

For Meditation: Isaiah 5:20

When I surrender to God's restrictions, I'm free to enjoy life the way he originally intended. *God, I will trust your viewpoint instead of my own on right versus wrong.*

Lesson 2: Kicking at Locked Doors
Read Genesis 3:1–6

BAIT. IT CAUSES victims to turn with fresh interest, luring them into a trap. It's wise for us to study the bait Satan laid out for Eve, because his methods haven't changed.

So what caused Eve to turn toward a tree she had not touched before now? Consider the first phrase Satan used: *"For God knows* that when you eat of it . . . you will be like God, *knowing* good and evil" (Gen. 3:5, emphasis added).

God knew something. He was hiding what he knew from Eve. That *hiddenness* was what Satan used as bait.

Control Girls detest being locked out or excluded. "Let me in there. Don't hide it from me!" we scream. But the only one who gets to see and know everything is God. He asked Eve to live her life brushing up against the Tree of the Knowledge of Good and Evil and remain at ease with not having its fruit or its knowledge. God didn't give an explanation. He wanted her to be content with not knowing why.

Satan wanted Eve *not* to be content. He portrayed the tree as a file cabinet behind the locked door of God's corner office, saying, "There are secret things behind that door. Hidden things. But this fruit will unlock the door."

How quickly Eve fell for Satan's bait. She ignored God's momentous warnings and hyper-focused on what he was hiding. With impetuous naïveté, Eve reached for the fruit like it was a stolen key, determined to unlock God's secrets.

LOCKED DOORS

I heard about a woman who returned home from work one day to have her visiting mother-in-law ask, "Why did you lock your bedroom door?"

The woman responded, "How did you know it was locked?"

Control Girls crave secret information. It's why we eavesdrop, read notes or texts that aren't addressed to us, or peek at diaries and letters.

We aren't content with what we don't know. We pick locks and steal keys. If we get frantic enough, we kick at the door. Why? *Because we want control*. If it's hidden, it's out of our control.

Sometimes, when we're concerned about someone we love, it's good and right to press for information. But God is in a class of his own. Think of it this way. You might put a tracker on your child's phone if you thought he was sneaking out. You might even kick in his door if you thought he was hiding something that could hurt him. But would you kick in the locked door of the Oval Office? I hope not! It would be disrespectful and inappropriate to demand that the president reveal secret information.

So then, is it fitting to kick at doors that God has locked, or demand that he give up hidden information? He's *God*. He doesn't answer to us. He sees things we can't, and he knows things we don't. Isaiah 55:9 says that God's thoughts are higher than our thoughts. His processing skills are infinitely more complex than ours.

Like he asked of Eve, God also asks that we trust him with what we can't see. Rather than kicking at locked doors, God invites us to "walk by faith, not by sight" (2 Cor. 5:7). **Faith is trusting that God is *for* us, even when he keeps things *from* us.**

But Satan's goal is to destroy our faith in God. He points to the door bolted shut between us and the supernatural realm and plants doubts about what God has hidden. He incites the sort of anger and distrust that says:

How could you let my husband get away with this affair?

Why am I still so lonely?

What kind of God allows a good person like Mom to suffer with cancer?

Why does my sister get new houses, and I get new mountains of debt?

It's not wrong to ask God questions, even angry ones. But it is wrong to *demand* answers. We don't always get to see God's purposes. He asks us to trust him and to have faith.

THE HIDDEN THINGS

Years ago, my husband, Ken, was ecstatic about a job offer from "Harold." Not only was the job a professional step up, it also offered an escape from a position Ken didn't love. With great excitement, we began planning for our long-distance move. Then suddenly, for no reason, Harold retracted the job offer.

Ken's enthusiasm instantly converted to profound disappointment. Continuing in his current position was a huge letdown, and he slipped into despondent gloom. I tried to get our Happy Ending back on track by ramping up an elaborate job search and reading Bible verses to Ken in rapid fire.

Nothing helped. I couldn't buoy Ken's spirits. I fretted about the stability of Ken's current position and worried he wouldn't find something new. I frantically wondered where this bend in our plans was leading. But by far my biggest frustration was *why*. "The job with Harold was so perfect, God," I wailed. "Why would you take it away?"

God began to answer that question a few months later with a phone call from my friend Jill. She didn't even say hello. She just blurted out, "God *protected* you, Shannon!"

Jill and her husband had initially connected us with Harold. They spoke so highly of him, I was convinced that Harold was God's answer to my prayers for a godly mentor for my husband. My viewpoint was a bit obstructed.

Jill's husband had just been fired, based on false accusations made by none other than Harold, which was our first clue that Harold was not who he seemed. Years later, Harold's fraudulent use of government funding came to light, along with a long list of sexual assault allegations. As I write, Harold is awaiting trial.

God protected us from a choice we surely would have regretted. What a faith-building experience, to get a glance at God's hand behind the locked door. God was for us, not against us!

Most of the time, though, God blocks our view into the supernatural realm. He doesn't allow us to see, because he wants us to have faith. He wants us to trust him with the hidden things and believe that he is good.

We can respond with skepticism and doubt, like Eve did, kicking at locked doors and demanding God give us answers. Or we can settle ourselves outside that locked door to the supernatural realm. We can brush up against what we don't know and remain at ease, knowing God is in control.

All of us have big, "But *why*, God?" moments in life. Even Jesus called out, "My God, my God, why have you forsaken me?" (Matt. 27:46). Giving up control means letting God decide what remains hidden. Friends, we have a God who is *for* us. Will we trust him with the hidden things?

❀ Recall your most recent, "But *why*, God?" moment. How was God asking you to relinquish control of the hidden things?

❀ What do you believe God currently wants you to be content *not* knowing? In what ways do you need to stop "kicking at locked doors"?

❀ Read John 20:29. What does Jesus say about those who don't see, yet believe? What would Jesus say about your faith?

For Meditation: Psalm 31:3–5

I can ask God questions, but it isn't my place to make demands. *God, I will stop kicking at locked doors and trust that you are for me.*

Lesson 3: Role-Playing
Read Genesis 2:15–3:7

WATCH CAREFULLY. THE most devastating scene in all of history is about to unfold. The stage is set. The spotlight shines brightly on the Tree of the Knowledge of Good and Evil. And now, the Serpent enters and swaggers right up to . . .

Wait. Eve? Something's up. God clearly made *Adam* the leader of his family. He created Adam first and gave him the tree rule before Eve was even created. Then God formed her out of Adam's rib and brought her to his side. Adam delighted in his wife and gave her a name. We can deduce that Adam also protectively warned her about the tree, since she knew of its peril.[1]

This backstory is what causes us to raise our eyebrows when we see Adam in the shadows for this highly dramatic scene. *Why isn't he center stage?* we wonder. Then we see.

This is Satan's way of insulting God. In essence, he's saying, *Oh yeah? You made him the leader? Well, watch this.*[2] No doubt, if God had made Eve the leader, Satan would have approached Adam. Whatever God establishes is what Satan wants to unravel. It's a control thing.

Eve, blissfully unaware of Satan's hostility toward God, is flattered by the attention. Satan makes her feel empowered and independent. The snake's sales pitch has her thinking about the exciting possibilities this fruit offers her family. So "she took of its fruit and ate, and she also gave some to her husband who was with her, and he ate" (Gen. 3:6).

Notice that they didn't both reach out and take the fruit. Eve initiated. She took the lead. And Adam passively followed. We can almost see Satan stepping behind the tree to do a fist pump. In one fell swoop, Satan incited Adam and Eve to reject both God's authority and his design for their marriage.

Satan incites us to do the same.

Passive Husbands

Take a quick glance around at the marriages you're privy to. Do you know any men tempted to be passive? Do you know any women tempted to undermine and emasculate? This pattern does not produce happy, resilient marriages. I know from experience. I naturally want to take control, and Ken naturally wants to let me. We strongly resemble Adam and Eve in this scene.

The text says Eve handed some fruit "to her husband who was with her" (v. 6), so we know that Adam was right there. When I read the scene, I want Adam to step in front of the Serpent and say, "Wait just a minute. If she eats that, she'll die! Honey, come behind me. This monster is trying to poison you!"

Instead, Adam is eerily silent, as are many husbands and fathers we know. Often a man is so absorbed with his work, his phone, or his game on TV that he's too distracted to notice when his sweet daughter walks out of the house with her bra showing beneath a sheer blouse. He's not even aware that his son is up in the bedroom feasting on porn or that his wife is addicted to steamy romance novels.

The husbands and fathers who opt out of leading on moral issues at home deeply impact both their families and our culture. But I think Control Girls have something to do with it too.

As a speaker, I love when women openly respond by nodding, smiling, or calling out from the audience. This encourages me to keep going and lets me know I'm connecting. The only time, however, I've had women call out *objections* from the audience is when I've said that Control Girls need to let their husbands lead. It's happened on at least three separate occasions. "What if he's too passive?" one hollered out. "What if he *won't* lead?" called another.

Oh, how my heart goes out to these women. I know that their blurted responses well up from deep frustration. Most of the women I meet really *want* their husbands to lead. We *tell* them to lead. We're incredibly irritated when they *don't* lead. But we don't know what to do about it.

Here is what I've learned: **If I take the lead, my husband probably won't**. Ken refuses to fight me for the reins. When he gets home after a day of challenging and pushing people at work, the last thing he wants to do is spar with me.

If I want control, he'll often give it to me, especially over little inconsequential decisions. I don't think it's wrong for me to pick out the new washing machine or hire the babysitter. But I notice that when I control lots of little things successively, a trend forms in my heart. I get used to deciding. I get used to not asking Ken's opinion. I get used to leading.

Like an alcoholic working at a bar, it's not good for me to have constant access to the control I wrongly crave. In control, I quickly become demanding, condescending, and rude toward my husband. But I can reverse the trend by warmly inviting Ken to lead. When I do, our home quickly settles back into a peaceful cadence.

Let me also add a note to my friends who embrace an egalitarian perspective of gender roles. Even if you think there should be no distinctions between the roles of husband and wife, the conclusion remains the same. By controlling your husband, you break your own rules for equality. To control him is to put him under your authority, which creates the same erosive tension.[3]

I Want a Hero

A while ago, my friend Jennifer asked me for some input on her marriage. As a busy mom of preschoolers, Jennifer felt like she was dangling by a thread. And like most damsels in distress, she wanted her husband to swoop in and rescue her. She wanted him to look deeply into her soul over a candlelit dinner for two and satisfy her craving for affection and adult conversation. But the more she pointed out his negligence, demanding he take her out or help with the kids, the more he retreated to the basement to do his own thing, which only infuriated her more.

Over the years, as Jennifer increasingly pushed the agenda, her husband had become reciprocally more passive. By the time they started a family, Jennifer had completely taken control. And now, with the third baby on the way, she was deeply dissatisfied with what their relationship had become.

What Jennifer was craving, I suggested, was not a guy in a cape to swoop in and help with her plans. What her heart longed for was a leader. But if she wanted him to lead, she'd need to stop controlling him.

Jennifer took my suggestion to heart. She began speaking to her husband as if he were the leader. Instead of being critical or demanding, she invited his input, even on little things. At one point, their two-year-old wasn't gaining weight, so Jennifer asked her husband, "What do you think we should try?" He suggested milk. Their older child hadn't been able to digest milk well, so Jennifer was predisposed to dismiss the idea. But responding to him as the leader, Jennifer said, "OK, I'll start giving her milk."

Well, guess who loved milk? Their baby girl drank it up with no problems and started gaining weight. Jennifer told her husband, "That was a really good idea!" As he got more involved in leading their family—even on little things like what to put in the sippy cup—Jennifer's husband was investing more. He suddenly *wanted* to help more. He felt needed. And since he was around more to notice all of the ways Jennifer was serving, it naturally made him want to lean over and give her a romantic kiss. (Which pretty much felt like him swooping in to rescue her from a tall building.)

When Jennifer took the lead, she caused her husband to feel irrelevant. But by respectfully honoring her husband's input and being leadable, she activated the hero-leader inside him. The Bible validates this chain reaction that Jennifer discovered. Have you noticed that the Bible always gives instructions to the wife first? It's because a husband can't follow his instructions until his wife follows hers. Ephesians 5:22–23 says, "Wives, submit to your own husbands, as to the Lord. For the husband is the head of the wife."

"Head" means leader. But here's what it doesn't mean: It does not mean that I'm to submit to all men—just my own husband. And it does not mean that I'm less capable of leading—the opposite may be true. It's out of respect for God and his design for marriage that I'm to defer to Ken.

Oh boy, this is a challenge for me, especially when I'm convinced that I'm right. Just last week, Ken cut in as I was (wrongly) lecturing our son, and said, "Shannon, stop." But I didn't *want* to stop. I had a fire in my belly and wanted to finish!

Submission is only submission when we *don't* agree on how to proceed. Reluctantly, I cut my lecture short and, as often happens, thirty minutes later I saw what I couldn't see in the moment: Ken was right. I was doing more harm than good.

Every time a Control Girl takes the lead and invites passivity in her husband, Satan does a fist pump. But in an exact reversal of the scene in the garden, when a woman respectfully submits to her husband, she activates the hero-leader inside him.

⚜ Do your tone and demeanor invite your husband to lead? Ask several family members what they think.

⚜ Do you see any correlation between your husband's passivity and your tendency to take control? How can you better draw out the leader in him?

⚜ In what ways do you feel more capable or competent than your husband? How can you, out of respect for God, defer to your husband? Pray for your husband, that he would lead your family well.

⚜ How can you encourage other wives to let their husbands lead?

For Meditation: Ephesians 5:22–23

If I continually take control at home, my husband probably won't fight me for the reins. *God, I will give you control of my marriage by inviting my husband to lead.*

Lesson 4: Cursed with a Craving
Read Genesis 3:8–24

EVE'S STORY, WHICH resembles a fairy tale in reverse, is devastatingly true. Her first bite into the fruit set something horrific into motion. We still live under its calamitous effects. One day, King Jesus will undo the sagging burden of the curse and restore creation to its glorious luster. But for now, each of us must contend with the evil that shattered our world in one juicy bite.

Imagine God's gravity as he approached Adam and Eve where they were busy hiding and blame-shifting under the strain of new guilt. With deep austerity, God pronounced judgments. One phrase in particular, directed toward Eve, has grave significance for Control Girls: "Your desire shall be for your husband, and he shall rule over you" (Gen. 3:16).

I always assumed this word "desire" carried a sexual connotation, but that never made sense to me. (I'll bet if we polled our husbands, they wouldn't consider increased sexual desire to be a curse.) To grasp what God meant, it's helpful to flip forward a chapter and examine the way God used the same wording as he warned Eve's son Cain: "Sin is crouching at the door. Its desire is for you, but you must rule over it" (Gen. 4:7).

So a woman will desire her husband in the same way that sin desired Cain—to overpower him and take control.[4] We could paraphrase God's words to Cain like this: "Sin has a desire, Cain. It wants to control you."[5]

If we take this meaning and apply it to the woman's curse, I could insert my name and say, "Shannon has a desire, Ken. She wants to control you."

UNDER THE CURSE

God designed for Eve to live happily under his reign and his design for her marriage. But Eve craved control. So God gave her over to both her desire and the misery it would produce.

She wanted control; God let her become controlling. Ray Ortlund calls God's judgment "a measure-for-measure response to [Eve's] sin."[6] So as a daughter of Eve, when I walked down the aisle with my white dress trailing behind, I also dragged into my marriage a desire for control.

For me, discovering that my control issues were seeded by the curse in Genesis 3 was like being diagnosed with a degenerative disease, passed on from generations back. Suddenly, my symptoms made sense. I always wondered why I was so combative and pugnacious toward the man I so deeply love. Now I understood. **As a daughter of Eve, I am infected with a desire to control.**

This is why I crouch like a tiger, waiting to pounce on my husband and get him to do things my way. It's why I talk over him, why I repeat myself until he caves in, why I say degrading things when he disagrees, and why I shame him when he displeases me.

When I live in this fallen way, my marriage also begins to parallel the second part of Eve's curse, which reads, "and he shall rule over you" (Gen. 3:16). Clawing after control does not draw out the protective leader in my husband. It doesn't build a friendship between two partners. Rather, it corrodes our relationship and sparks hostility between us.

As we know, this strife and struggle between men and women isn't confined to marriage. Broadly speaking, both men and women tend to ignore their own weaknesses and exploit the weaknesses of the other sex.

Fallen men tend to be emotionally distant, guarded, and insensitive. Men ignore their families and become workaholics. Daddies fail to hug their little girls or say "I love you" to their sons. Husbands whistle at attractive women in front of their wives.

In their most depraved, selfish state, men exploit the vulnerability of women and are abusive and demeaning. They rape, beat, abandon, objectify, and degrade women. The harsh effect of dominant men on the world is staggering.

Fallen women also contribute to the Battle of the Sexes. Women tend to be overly sensitive and punish men with emotional outbursts. Wives hold on to offenses and become bitter. A woman intuitively knows how to exploit a man's weakness. She uses his lust against him by leveraging her sexual appeal. She knows how deeply he craves respect and uses that against him too. She might not be able to pin him down physically, but she can break him down with mockery, demeaning disrespect, or public emasculation.

Our culture is quick to condemn the sinful, abusive man—and we should be. But we're often quite reluctant to criticize the sinful, controlling woman. Given all that women have to contend with—abuse, mistreatment, and inequality—we tend to sanction or justify a woman's controlling behavior. We laugh when an elderly woman shakes her cane in the face of a security guard. We high-five the little girl who says she'll never need a man.

Our culture celebrates women who are strong and independent and who rise up to take control. We're told the world would fall into a peaceful cadence, if only women would be more forceful and men would be more passive. And yet, this pattern never seems to heal *my* marital conflict.

A BAGEL BATTLE

A year or so ago, on a sunny morning, my husband and I spontaneously stopped for bagels. We chatted congenially in line, and when it was our turn, the teen behind the counter asked for our order. I said cheerfully, "I'll have two blueberry, two cranberry walnut . . ."

My husband cut in and said, "Get some whole wheat." I told him I was going to add those at the end and started over. "I'll have two blueberry, two cranberry walnut . . ."

Again my husband cut in, "I think Cade would like chocolate chip." I sighed and began again, "I'll have two blueberry, two cranberry walnut . . ."

A third time, he cut in, asking if there was a special on cream cheese.

Usually Ken hates to order. He can't keep straight what everyone likes, and it irritates him when we all call out our preferences. Now suddenly *he* was the one with the preferences, and *I* was getting irritated. So I took a step back, folded my arms, and said, "Go ahead," with a nod toward the counter.

Ken stepped back too, and said, "No way. I'm not ordering."

So there we stood, like two stubborn children, dressed as grown-ups, refusing to order. The kid behind the counter just wanted *somebody* to order. So what mature, reasonable thing did I do? I turned on my heel and left the only grown-up standing in line to order. Five minutes later, Ken got in the car with his bag of bagels, fuming. "You just *left* me there!" he said.

"Seemed like you were doing just fine on your own."

Ken sighed and shook his head. "After seventeen years of marriage, we can't even order bagels together."

This struck us both as funny, partly because it was so true. We can take even the sunny task of ordering bagels and turn it into a battle. Notice how my desire for control kicked in? With assertive, condescending demeanor, I took control back, and left my well-meaning husband stranded. In my fallen ugliness, my desire for control can infect even the most carefree moments of the day.

My culture may cheer me on when I'm pushy, independent, demanding, and domineering, but when I turn on my heel and bring these attitudes to my marriage or other relationships, I inevitably drive in wedges. The more controlling I get, the less happy we all are.

God provides a better way. Rather than scrapping the sin-dilapidated version of marriage, God restores marriages like mine. He invites wives and husbands to serve each other, guided by God's original blueprint for marriage.

Yes, I am infected with a desire for control. But God wants to reverse the curse in my heart and in my relationships—and in yours. Will we let him?

* ❀ Are you a controlling, pushy woman? How does understanding the curse help you discern your sin?

* ❀ Compare Colossians 3:12–15 to your closest relationships. How have these relationships been infected by your desire for control?

For Meditation: Romans 8:20–21

I am infected with a desire for control that leads to misery, not happiness. *God, please reverse the curse of control in my heart and in my relationships. I surrender to your work in my life.*

Eve's Happy Ending

EVE'S FAIRY TALE in reverse is still awaiting its Happy Ending. We groan under God's judgment, hampered with our desire for control. But in his mercy, God has made a way for Control Girls to reverse the curse. He invites us to live by faith, not sight. To let him determine what is good. To embrace his design for marriage. And to welcome the rule of Jesus, our Prince of Peace, who heals our blighted hearts and brings all things back under his control.

Chapter Three
Sarah: It's Up to Me

🌼 SARAH'S STORY in the Bible is mostly told in the margins of her husband's story. Abraham was the great man of faith who left everything behind and stepped out into the wild unknown, tethered only by some massive promises from God, which all seemed to hang on the arrival of his first baby.

Sarah lived under the decades-long humiliation of not being able to produce this baby. Through all of Sarah's frustration and pain, God was there, with a Happy Ending in store. He told her it was coming. He was just waiting for the right moment to bless her with it.

Lesson 1: God's Barricading Hand
Read Genesis 16:1–6

MY HUSBAND WAS just as happy to send out a pink birth announcement as the blue ones. He's not concerned about the Popkin name carrying into the next century. And at some point (hopefully before they turn forty) he expects our kids' rooms to be empty.

Husbands of Sarah's* day had different expectations. Children were assets. They were your labor force and retirement fund all wrapped up into one little, nursing baby. Boy babies were far better than girls, because you didn't exchange them for a measly dowry; you got to keep them. When the boys married, they pitched their tent right next door. Every drop of their sweat went into protecting and providing for the collective good of the clan—*your* clan.

So everybody wanted boys. Men wanted their wives to deliver baby boys, and wives wanted to prove their worth by doing just that—as many times as possible. Any Control Girl of that day would have been fixated on one goal: having baby boys.

Sarah was no exception; her life ambition was to be a mother. Yet after a lifetime of trying, she was still clogging up the family business profit flow, first with her monthly periods and then with no periods at all. She was like a production line in a plant that had been shut down, or a cash crop that had rotted thirty years in a row.

SARAH'S HUMILIATION

Just for a moment, suppose that, rather than being childless, Sarah was obese, bald, deeply scarred, and disfigured. If this seems more shameful to you than being childless, it's because you wear the glasses of your own culture, which emphasizes beauty over fertility.

For Sarah, it was the reverse. To be childless was utterly humiliating. To make matters worse, Sarah's husband had unwavering faith in God's

---

* In today's Scripture reading, you see the names Abram and Sarai; God eventually changed their names to Abraham and Sarah, which is what I'll be calling them.

promise to give him more descendants than the stars in the sky. God had said, "Your very own son shall be your heir" (Gen. 15:4).

This was astonishingly good news to Abraham. But for Sarah, it added even more humiliation. It was like the obese, bald, scarred woman's husband believing she had a future in modeling. Abraham's faith in God only made Sarah feel more exposed and ashamed. She couldn't do what they were expecting.

RESPONDING TO GOD

Ten years went by. A decade of compounding shame and anxiety that God could have prevented. Sarah recognized that the door to pregnancy had been sealed off by God's own hand, and there was nothing she could do to pry it open. So she said to Abraham, "Behold now, the LORD has prevented me from bearing children. Go in to my servant; it may be that I shall obtain children by her" (Gen. 16:2).

We'll talk more about Sarah's alternative plan in lesson 2, but for now, let's think carefully about Sarah's response to God. She saw God's hand as the barricade, preventing what she longed for. Yet rather than trusting God's hand, Sarah took matters into her own Control Girl hands.

As women, we are incredibly committed to making things turn out right for our families. We pry open doors that everybody says are locked. We overcome obstacles that others label impossible. We are relentless and resolute. Our tenacity is what makes us exceptional.

But when it's *God's* hand barricading the path, our relentless tenacity is not admirable. In fact, **by persistently going around his hand, God says we have turned *against* him**.

Now, this isn't how we would interpret our own bullheadedness. Sarah actually thought she was *underwriting* God's plan. God was the one promising future generations. Sarah was just providing the second wife to make it happen. She saw herself as the benefactor—the one paying for the family line to be extended.

In one sense, this was true. Hagar was Sarah's personal asset. Per the customs of the day, Sarah would present any child Hagar delivered to

Abraham as her own. She was simply cashing in some property to make God's promise come true.

But that's just the thing. God doesn't want us making his promises come true. He wants us waiting on him. God was tenderly cultivating a Happy Ending for Sarah that was more richly satisfying than anything she could ever come up with on her own. But all Sarah saw was the cold harshness of God's barricading hand. Listen to how these verses echo Sarah's heart:

> He has walled me about so that I cannot escape; . . .
> though I call and cry for help,
>   he shuts out my prayer. (Lam. 3:7–8)

Sometimes God's hand prevents the thing we long for. Other times, his hand doesn't stop the thing we dread. But always God offers these cord-dangling moments as opportunities to renew our hope in him alone. When our illusion of control is either shattered or dries up over time, we have a choice. Will we circumvent God's hand like Sarah did? Or will we fling ourselves *into* his hands and surrender our sorrow to him?

TWO HURTING MOMS

I heard about a mom whose teenage son was killed in a car accident. Over time, her devastation and grief turned to rage—not just against the drunk driver who had ended her son's life, but against God, who could have prevented it. She went from being integrally involved in her church to abandoning her faith. After years of fighting for maximum sentencing and raising awareness with her angry voice, she still has no relief. Her endless rant only chains her to vengeance and grief.

I watched another woman I know lose her little girl to leukemia. It was devastating. Julie was a delight to her family. When Julie died, her mom longed to go dig up her grave. She just wanted to hold her baby one more time. But as the years continued to pass, this sweet mama started to smile again. If you met her today, she would talk fondly of Julie and remind you that leukemia isn't what took Julie to heaven. It was the trusted hand of Jesus.

From where I stand, this woman seems free. She made it through a trial I can't even imagine facing. But her unfettered faith in God gives me hope.

What's the difference between these two grieving moms? I think it's what they did with their *lack* of control. One pounded her fists angrily against God's hand, determined not to surrender to him. The other mom relinquished her devastation to God. She didn't grieve any less. She just grieved differently. Perhaps she began with her fists pounding against God, but eventually she let his hand envelop both her and her little girl.

Control Girl, is God barricading off one of your dreams for a Happy Ending? If so, you have a choice. You can circumvent God's hand like Sarah did. Or you can fling yourself *into* God's mighty hands, knowing he cares for you.

❀ Tell about a way God has wedged his hand between you and a dream. How have you responded?

❀ How does Lamentations 3:1–9 mirror your experience?

❀ Now read Lamentations 3:19–26. Apply the words of truth as a balm to soothe your suffering. How can you put your problem and solution in God's hands instead of your own?

For Meditation: Psalm 32:8–10

By pushing against God's hand or going around it, I turn myself against him. *God, rather than circumventing your hand, I will fling myself into your hands and surrender my sorrows to you.*

Lesson 2: God's Voice Versus Mine
Read Genesis 16:1–4

THERE'S A PHRASE in Sarah's story that reminds us of Eve's story. Notice the similarities:

- "Because you have listened to the voice of your wife and have eaten of the tree . . ." (Gen. 3:17).
- "And Abram listened to the voice of Sarai" (Gen. 16:2).

Now, usually, when a husband listens to his wife, we think of it as a good thing, but not this time. Why? Because both Eve and Sarah were talking their husbands out of following God's directions.

In both instances, the husband (and not the wife) was given direct instruction from God. Before Eve was even created, God warned Adam about the tree. They were not to eat of it or they would die (Gen. 3:17). Without Sarah present, God gave Abraham distinct promises about the future: Abraham would have a son, and his family of two would become a nation destined to fill the land of Canaan and bless the whole world (Gen. 12:3; 15:18).

Both times, God instructed the husband, expecting him to lead his family. And both times, the wife cut in with a rerouted plan. The wife talked, the husband listened, and the family headed off course.

In James 3, the tongue is compared to the rudder of a ship. Words can reroute. They have that power. And it's clear that God has gifted women, in particular, with words. It takes but a few moments with a group of preschoolers to notice how God has equipped most little girls with skills for communication and relationship. While the boys will likely have their heads down, building things and making truck noises, the girls will likely be in pairs, expressively sharing ideas. They'll be facing each other and communicating whole ranges of emotions.

These differences we often see in boys and girls are by God's design. God gives each woman—with her abilities to relate, communicate, and express emotion—as a gift to her family. To make my point, picture your next family gathering if the women only contributed in the way the men usually do. Perhaps there wouldn't *be* a gathering. See what a difference we make? We draw people together and help relationships to flourish.

But Control Girls often wrongly leverage these gifts. We're gifted for relationships, so we use our relational ties and influence to drive our own agendas. We know who to push, how hard, and when. We're also gifted communicators, so we argue and advocate for our ideas. We talk behind backs, repeat divisive comments, and leverage conflict between others to get what we want.

Like Eve and Sarah, we can use our tongues as powerful rudders to steer and redirect the people we have influence over. This is especially true with our husbands. Often, we're so convinced that we can captain our family's ship better than our husbands, we talk until they listen. But God wants us to watch *him* lead our husbands in the direction our family should go.

When Abraham left his homeland, "He went out, not knowing where he was going" (Heb. 11:8). So, without Sarah even suggesting a left turn, God directed Abraham from Ur to Canaan. Just as God led Abraham then, he wanted to lead Abraham now. But Sarah was talking over the voice of God.

She said, "Have sex with my servant. I'll get a baby that way." Though this was culturally acceptable at the time, it was not the faith-inspired path God had called Abraham to. It was a path of compromise proposed by a woman who was sick of waiting on God.

Happily Ever After-the-Addition

Years ago, I began complaining that our kitchen was too small. We only had room for a small table, which wasn't nearly big enough to host large dinner parties. I told my husband that putting an addition on the back of our house would solve all of our problems. But he wasn't aware that we *had* any problems. (He didn't really want to host dinner parties.)

To be fair, I should note that Ken did not drag me into our small-kitchened house kicking and screaming. Actually, I told him it was my "Happily Ever After" house. But now I was thinking "Happily Ever After-the-Addition."

I kept showing Ken new sketches, complete with window seats and built-in shelves. But Ken never caught the vision. The more elaborate my drawings and ideas, the quieter he became. After months of me talking, Ken finally caved and agreed to the addition. More accurately, he agreed to begin *saving* for the addition. He figured that in five or six years we could afford to rip the back off our house and build the kitchen of my dreams. I was elated, except for the six-year part. In six years, the kids would be half grown. So I secretly looked for an acceleration plan.

After a couple years of saving, we got a triple-decker surprise. Within a week's time, we received a large gift from Ken's parents, an unexpected tax return, and a big, fat bonus check.

When Ken suggested we go out for dinner to discuss how we would use the money, I smiled secretly to myself. *He must not realize I'm pretty good at math*, I chortled. I already had it figured out. The combined amount was *exactly* what we still lacked for the addition! Who could deny that this was the Lord's will?

Seated across from me at the restaurant, Ken grinned widely, and then slid a spreadsheet across the table. "What's this?" I asked, skimming the rows.

There were several missionaries and nonprofit organizations listed, each with numbers beside them. Big numbers. My heart sank fast as my eyes scanned the page, searching for the addition. There it was, way at the bottom, with a little number beside it. The same number as last year.

Looking up, I realized two things. Ken hadn't even considered putting the extra money toward the addition. And he had no idea I was counting on it.

Clearly, Ken has the spiritual gift of giving. He gets so excited about opportunities to give. I ordinarily *want* God to direct and use my husband. But rather than seeing this spreadsheet as tangible proof that God was doing just that, I saw it as tangible proof that Ken didn't want me to have my addition. Ken was listening to God, but I wanted him listening to *me*.

The argument that ensued was the type to make a waitress turn around and come back later. I leaned forward, my eyes blazing. "Ken," I seethed, "do you know that it's not *wrong* to spend our own money?"

He was stunned. He kept shaking his head, and repeating in bewilderment, "Honey, I thought we agreed that the addition was something we were *saving* for . . ." Our evening out ended with slammed car doors and terse silence. Ken's enthusiasm over the gifts turned to glum frustration, and I initiated an icy silence that lasted for days.

But slowly, steadily, God thawed my heart. I saw how wrong I had been. I repented before the Lord with many tears and humbly asked Ken to forgive me, which he graciously did.

I still wanted the addition desperately, but even more, I wanted God to direct my husband. I wholeheartedly supported his plans for the money and even helped the kids draw pictures to go into the envelopes for the missionaries and organizations. The gifts went out, and I had a settled peace.

We never did build the addition, but we did hear some amazing stories of how God used our gifts. One missionary said it met their need to the dollar.

A year later, we moved to a new house that, in hindsight, was clearly God's plan for us all along. I got a bigger kitchen and, more importantly, a bigger understanding of how God uses my husband to direct our family.

Like with Adam and Abraham, God gives unique clarity, perspective, and understanding to husbands. He gives specific direction to Ken that he purposefully doesn't give to me. **I need to stop talking, badgering, and pressuring with my agenda long enough for my husband to hear God's agenda.** This doesn't mean I can't give input or share my ideas, but I must be wary of my temptation to take control.

When Sarah talked Abraham into sleeping with Hagar, she steered her family straight into uncharted, choppy waters that would eventually bring more pain and sorrow than she could have ever foreseen. Dear wives, let's learn from Sarah's grave mistake, shall we? Let's encourage our husbands (and others) to listen for God's voice, not just our own.

❀ What are you currently trying to talk someone, specifically your
    husband, into? List any situations in which you suspect someone
    is listening to your voice instead of God's. How can you encourage
    others to be led by God?

❀ Read Proverbs 21:9 and 19. Do you badger your husband or oth-
    ers, pushing for your agenda? Keep tabs on your tongue over the
    next twenty-four hours. Consider how keeping quiet is a way to
    relinquish control to God.

For Meditation: John 10:27

I need to stop talking, badgering, and pressuring with my agenda
so that others can hear God's agenda. *God, I believe that it is far better for*
___Patrick___ *to hear your voice than mine.*

God, please direct my husband. Give
me wisdom to know when to
shut up. Give him a clear path
to leading our marriage, our home,
the worship team.

Lesson 3: Hell Hath No Fury
Read Genesis 16:1–6

SARAH THOUGHT NOTHING could be worse than decades of infertility, but she was wrong. There's *one* thing worse: being scorned by the woman who's having your husband's baby.

Sarah had imagined finally garnering honor and dignity, receiving gifts for the baby, and congratulations from the neighbors. This pregnancy was supposed to *relieve* Sarah of humiliation, not incite more. Yet any last embers of Sarah's dignity were being stamped out beneath Hagar's feet as she pranced about in maternity clothes and shot condescending glances Sarah's way. *How dare she.*

Imagine the emotions churning in Sarah's infertile belly as she replayed Hagar's looks of contempt in her mind. What did this smugness imply? What had Abraham said to Hagar to embolden her and instill such entitlement? And what was Abraham saying about *Sarah*? Was his pleasure over a coming heir tangled up in the pleasure of sleeping with this *slave*? What promises had he whispered into Hagar's ear as they embraced? What did this woman, who now carried Abraham's seed, mean to him?

Sarah was in a painfully vulnerable position. It was all out of her control.

THE UGLINESS OF CONTROL

Prepare yourself. We're about to get a good look at the underbelly of our desire for control. It won't be pretty. But if we are serious about reversing the curse, we must.

As Hagar gloats, we expect Sarah to turn at any moment on the "other woman," wrath spewing. And she will, but not yet. First, she flies at her husband, the man who's letting it all happen.

"I gave my servant to your embrace," Sarah sneers (Gen. 16:5). A literal translation would read: "I put my slave-girl in your lap," which is a euphemism for the genital area.[1] Sarah wouldn't have used such crass language lightly. These are powerhouse words. Then she deals the final blow: "May the LORD judge between you and me!" (v. 5).

Judges are the people who bang gavels and hand out verdicts. And Sarah wants verdicts. Conveniently forgetting her role in giving Hagar to Abraham, she wants to play the victim. If she can persuade Abraham that he's the guilty party, then she's in control and can demand restitution.

A CONTROL GIRL VICTIM

After forty years of marriage, Catherine was outraged to learn that her husband was having an affair. Her adult children weren't surprised, though. They had watched their mom criticize and emasculate their dad for decades, so the idea of him looking outside his marriage for companionship wasn't outlandish. They deeply sympathized with Catherine, and they didn't *excuse* their dad, but they did pity him.

Well, this didn't sit well with Catherine. She was irate. How could her children not see her as the sole victim? How could they reduce their dad's guilt? In a grand attempt to deflect responsibility for the marriage problems and solicit undivided support from her children, Catherine did something drastic. She tried to take her own life, or at least go to the brink. But since the drugs she took can't actually kill a person, her kids interpreted even her suicide attempt as yet another desperate control tactic.

Catherine's story shows just how far we Control Girls will go to deflect responsibility and claim victim status. Sarah's story makes the same point.

As you recall, Sarah didn't just give Abraham reason to look outside their marriage; she set up the date with the other woman. Yet now she's spewing accusations about Abraham enjoying a lap dance at her expense! Sarah wants to be labeled the victim because she feels so vulnerable. What she's craving is control.

AN INDIFFERENT HUSBAND

Abraham responded the way many husbands do when their wives spew scalding accusations: he did nothing. Rather than providing loving leadership by sorting out this painful situation between his two wives, Abraham opts out, saying, "Behold, your servant is in your power; do to her as you please" (Gen. 16:6). He tells his Control Girl to take control.

I can't decide whether to picture Abraham casually glancing up from his newspaper as he says this, or spitefully sneering in Sarah's face. Either way, Sarah finds his response deeply unsatisfying. Ironically, she didn't want to be told to take control.

What an ugly, distorted picture of what God designed a marriage to be! The husband is abdicating his role of leader and protector. The wife is taking control. And everyone is suffering as they live out the curse.

An Abusive Control Girl

What happens next is as ugly as any Control Girl scene in the Bible. Sarah digs in her heels, determined that she *will* take control. And she does so with vengeance: "Then Sarai dealt harshly with [Hagar], and she fled from her" (Gen. 16:6).

This word *harshly* is the same word used in Exodus when the Egyptians oppressed the Hebrew people and made them their slaves. (Which is an interesting reversal since, here, it's a Hebrew oppressing an Egyptian.) We don't know exactly what Sarah's harshness entailed, but it was severe enough to cause a pregnant girl to take her chances alone in the desert. We catch our breath, asking, "Sarah, how could you justify such scandalous behavior?"

Here's how: all along, Sarah has fixated on the wrong done *to her*. Never mind that Hagar was a slave obeying her bedroom assignment. Rather than sorting out the blame, Sarah wanted to bang God's gavel and hand out verdicts. She's the obvious victim, since she's suffering while everyone else is quite pleased with themselves. Well, someone was going to pay.

If Abraham wanted to wave the red cape and sidestep while Sarah charged at him, then she would just follow his lead and point her horns at the slave instead. She might get Abraham to wince a little too, as she bruised up his new mama.

Ultimately, Sarah was on a rampage to get what all abusers want: control.

A SELF-VICTIMIZING ABUSER

Perhaps Sarah didn't care whether she was right or wrong, but there's a good chance, as she raised her hand over Hagar, that Sarah was seeing herself as the victim.[2] Self-victimization is actually common among abusers. Rather than taking responsibility for the shattered glass or your broken nose, an abuser will fly into a rage and say, "It's your fault. You're the one who made me mad!"

Oh, how disastrously blind we can be to our own sin. **We become so fixated on the wrong done *to* us that we fail to see the wrong we've committed against others.** We can spend our whole lives charging down the path of a Control Girl, never realizing that our lust for control is turning us, slowly but surely, into ugly, shameful women.

But God points us in a new direction. God wants us to confess our sin and make things right. Now, these instructions seem awfully counterintuitive to a Control Girl who has fixated on the wrong done to her. But they lead to freedom and peace.

What might have happened if Sarah had humbled herself before God and apologized to Abraham for her lack of faith? Taking responsibility for our contribution to a difficult situation is never easy. It's far less painful to bang God's gavel and find labels like "emotional abuser" or "narcissist" for the people who have hurt us.[3] And while others are probably wrong, oftentimes we are too.

It's a matter of relinquishing control to say, "I was wrong. Will you forgive me? Let me make this right." Those words have the power to break sin's grasp on *me*. Confession cleanses me of my controlling heart. It's a powerful way to put God in charge of my Happy Ending.

⁂ How have you abused someone else in an effort to get control? Don't limit your scope to the type of abuse that people go to jail for. Have you given someone the "silent treatment"? Withheld affection? Turned others against someone? Write out a plan with a deadline to make this right.

❋ Have you ever made yourself the victim to avoid being confronted with your own sin? What is God convicting you of? How can you relinquish control and make this situation right?

For Meditation: Proverbs 17:15, 20

When I fixate on the wrong done to me, I fail to see the wrong I've committed against others. *God, I confess my own sin of* _____ *to you. Please cleanse my heart of control.*

Lesson 4: Never Too Old to Become Beautiful
Read Genesis 18:1–15; 21:1–7

GIVEN FULL VENT, my desire for control will take me further into sin than I ever wanted to go. It will make me uglier than I ever imagined I could be. And it will fill my life with more devastation than I thought possible. Sarah's story has demonstrated this very colorfully.

But the best part of Sarah's story is that it doesn't end ugly. I love how the apostle Peter, when scanning the Old Testament in search of a beautiful, quiet, submissive woman for us to emulate, chooses Sarah. (Read what Peter wrote in 1 Peter 3:3–6.)

PROFILING SARAH

Now, I have to admit, when I first studied Sarah's life in detail, I was a little perturbed by Peter's choice. Sarah? A gracious, quiet, submissive wife? I didn't think she was.

No doubt, Peter's choice was owing to the *end* of Sarah's story. Perhaps Peter was partial to stories with grand reversals, since his own story included a triple betrayal of Christ followed by a critical role in the early church.

Sarah had a grand reversal too. She went from being ashamed, despondent, and abusive to having strong, beautiful faith. And she did so at age eighty-nine. Hebrews 11:11 describes the moment Sarah's story took that hairpin turn: "By faith Sarah herself received power to conceive, even when she was past the age, since she considered him faithful who had promised."

Hebrews 11 is the great hallmark chapter of faith, commemorating people who took drastic measures to follow God. So why was Sarah included? Once again, I was skeptical. James 2:26 says, "Faith apart from works is dead," and Hebrews 11 emphasizes this concept by listing amazing acts of faith. Noah built his boat. Abraham offered up Isaac. Moses parted the Red Sea. But Sarah? Sarah didn't *do* anything that gave evidence of her faith, did she?

After taking another look, I discovered that Sarah did *do* something requiring great faith. This act marks the grand reversal in Sarah's story and the point where she goes from being ugly and controlling to surrendered and beautiful in God's sight.

What did Sarah do? She slept with Abraham.

NOTHING IS IMPOSSIBLE

In Genesis 18, we find eighty-nine-year-old Sarah listening from behind a tent flap as her husband shares lunch with a visitor (who happens to be God). Imagine her surprise when *she* becomes the topic of conversation. Within a year, the visitor predicts, Sarah will have a baby. Clearly this visitor hadn't seen her white hair.

The idea was so preposterous that Sarah laughed to herself, saying, "At my age—old and decrepit, as is my husband—both of us long past having any desire to engage in lovemaking?" (Gen. 18:12 VOICE).

As Sarah gives commentary on her sex life, we can be sure she wasn't talking out loud.[4] And yet, the visitor heard her. He asked why Sarah laughed.

It would seem that Sarah was summoned from the tent to *face* their guest, since after she denied laughing, the Lord spoke directly to her. "No, but you did laugh," he said (Gen. 18:15).

I wonder if there was a twinkle in God's eye as he said it. Before him was a little, old woman who long ago had dreamed of mothering to life a family as numerous as the stars. Her dream had dried up decades ago, along with her womb, and yet now God planned to bring the dream—and her womb—to life again. According to his original plan, God was going to fill this woman's aching, wrinkled arms with a baby.

I imagine gentleness in God's tone when he said, "Is anything too hard for the LORD?" (Gen. 18:14). It's the same message the angel gave Mary when she wondered how a virgin might bear a son (Luke 1:35–37).

How Sarah's pulse must have quickened over the months to come whenever she turned this phrase over in her mind. Was anything too difficult for the Lord? That was the question.

PASSIONATE FAITH

Sarah might be embarrassed at the way we're listening in on her private thoughts. But when she says that she's long past having any desire for lovemaking, she gives us an important detail: she and Abraham weren't sleeping together anymore. Which places even greater significance upon what she's about to do.

Over the past half century, Sarah's hope for conceiving a baby had slipped away like trickles of water into desert sand. Any reserved droplets of hope must have evaporated at the sound of Ishmael's first cry. Hagar had given Abraham a son. God's promise had been fulfilled.

For Sarah to hope for a baby at age eighty-nine, after a lifetime of infertility, was preposterous. It would be like me, at age forty-four, after a lifetime of not being able to do a back handspring, hoping to become an Olympic gymnast. That window of opportunity has been closed. Painted shut. Boarded over. Imagine how foolish I would look, showing up in my leotard at the US Olympic trials.

I assure you that Sarah felt every bit as foolish as this when she considered sliding into bed next to Abraham. They weren't having sex anymore. And to have sex because they were trying for a *baby*? *Really*? This plan required great faith. The active kind.

The moment Sarah conceived Isaac was undeniably an incredible moment of surrender. Sarah wasn't trying to control anything; she knew this was completely *out* of her control.

So, I have put my skepticism to rest. Not only does Sarah deserve her place in Hebrews 11, she also earned Peter's honorable mention. She truly is a beautiful example of a woman sweetly surrendered to God.

As promised, Sarah gave birth to her long-awaited son, about one year after the Lord came to lunch. Holding her newborn miracle, Sarah said, "God has made laughter for me" (Gen. 21:6). It's a pun, since Isaac's name means "laughter." Surely God *did* create this sweet laughter.

SURRENDER

When we picture surrendering to God, I think we sometimes picture a dreary, uphill climb. And many times it is. But our mental image of surrendering to God should also include a picture of Sarah holding Isaac on her lap, for it was surrender that brought this "Laughter" to life.

Picture Sarah's eyes dancing with delight as she cups the feathery head of her newborn boy. Picture her calling Abraham over to witness his first smile. Picture her hooking his chubby fingers over his daddy's big, weathered one. Listen to Sarah giggle as she leans down to rub her nose against her baby's cheek. Listen to her husband chuckle at the sight of Sarah's gray curls against the fresh baby skin. Listen to the deep, hearty laugh of God, as he looks on.

Surrender to God is what makes us beautiful. And we're never too old to be enhanced with this sort of beauty. As we leave behind our haggish, controlling ways, we give God the opportunity to delight us with gifts that we could never have imagined. To surrender to God brings laughter to life.

❀ What problem seems too difficult, even for God? How would a response of surrender differ from control?

❀ Make a list of what you most fear or dread. How should you respond to this list, based on 1 Peter 3:6? How would a desire for control lead you differently?

❀ How does the end of Sarah's story reshape your view of God? Does surrender to him seem a little less burdensome? What does your answer reveal about your own faith? Journal your thoughts.

For Meditation: Hebrews 11:11

Rather than dreading the dreary, uphill challenge of surrender, I must remember that I'm surrendering to the God who brings laughter to life. *God, I trust that you will use the struggle of surrender to make me beautiful.*

Lesson 5: A Family Threat
Read Genesis 21:8–14

WHEN THE BIG boys won't let my child on the slide. When the text invite went to everyone but my daughter. When the substitute teacher didn't let my child eat his lunch. Nothing gives rise to my inner Control Girl like a bully messing with my kids.

For Sarah, this happened at a party for her son, Isaac. The whole clan had gathered to celebrate the little boy named "Laughter," and though Sarah was laughing more easily than she had in decades, she wasn't laughing now.

It's because Ishmael, Hagar's teenage son, was laughing *at* Isaac.

Holidays and celebrations, with all of their added pressures and expectations, don't always bring out the best in a Control Girl. Plus, Sarah had the added tension of the "other woman" attending this party. So it's not surprising that Sarah erupts over her son being teased by the big kids. What is surprising, though, is her severity.

Sarah steps protectively in front of her precious boy and says to Abraham, "Cast out this slave woman with her son, for the son of this slave woman shall not be heir with my son Isaac" (Gen. 21:10). Sarah doesn't just want to show them the door. She wants them gone forever. Pretty drastic, right?

A Threatened Inheritance

Now, before we roll our eyes or downplay the threat, let's listen to Sarah's reasoning. She believes Ishmael is going to steal Isaac's inheritance.

She's in her nineties, remember, so she's more apt to be thinking about estate planning. And the scene she just witnessed—with Ishmael bullying her son—is perhaps something of an epiphany. Sarah realizes that the tension between these two half brothers isn't going to melt on its own. Ishmael, who thinks of himself as Abraham's firstborn heir, is never going to back down, especially not after Abraham and Sarah are gone.[5]

But let's remember that Sarah didn't give Isaac firstborn rights—God did. Before Isaac was even born, God clarified that his promises were intended for Sarah's son, not Hagar's (Gen. 17:21). So by wanting to kick them to the curb, Sarah isn't just having a mama bear moment. She's finally seeing Ishmael for what he truly is—a threat to her family's inheritance.

In Galatians 4, Paul has a "mama bear" moment too. He steps out in front of us—God's children—and insists that our bully be kicked to the curb. To make his point, Paul brings up this incident between Sarah and Hagar. Hagar, he says, represents what can be produced without God. Her baby was conceived in self-reliance. But Sarah represents what only God can produce. Her baby was conceived in faith.

Paul tells us, "Don't let yourselves be bullied by these Ishmael-types who say you have to slave away under a list of rules. Ishmael was the guy who *didn't* get the inheritance, remember? You're like Isaac—born into God's family through faith. It wasn't self-reliance that made you God's child; it was God doing a miracle in your heart."

Paul says we should be like Sarah, who said, "Cast out the slave woman and her son" (Gal. 4:30).

Sarah's response seems drastic, but if Ishmael had stayed, he would have posed a continuous threat to Isaac's inheritance. It's ironic, really. Ishmael was Sarah's idea in the first place. Fifteen years ago, she was the one urging her husband to sleep with Hagar. So unwittingly, Sarah invited this threat into her home. And perhaps we do the same.

MY FAMILY'S INHERITANCE

I have a grave concern for Control Girls. **I think controlling women produce some of the godliest *looking* families in the church.** In our cunning way, we can twist Scripture into a whip on our kids' backs. We can make our husbands squirm under our condemning glare. We can prod and punish and prompt until our family members cave in to the pressure and eke out the polished Christian personae we had in mind.

And what is our goal? We want our loved ones to inherit the future that God promises his children. We want them to have heaven. The threat of family members *not* joining God's family ignites our inner Control Girl!

But here's my concern: What if we're producing slaves, not sons?

Jesus said, "The slave does not remain in the house forever; the son remains forever" (John 8:35). Ishmael certainly proved those words true. He was cast out with no inheritance.

Quite frankly, a Control Girl mom can produce a pretty convincing imitation Christian, and this she can do *without God*. But a true child of God—one who gets the inheritance—can't be produced by a controlling mom. His birth into God's family is like the birth of Isaac. It involves a miracle, performed by God and no one else.

This is so difficult for me. What if I have a mouthy, lazy teenager? A sneaky preschooler? What if my husband watches sports all weekend? Or my child lies? As a Control Girl, I have a whole litany of tactics to unleash on these ungodly habits in my home. But when I succeed in obliterating the unruliness I see in my family, have I produced something genuine and true? Or have I simply succeeded in gaining control?

According to Barna Group's research, nearly six in ten Millennials who grew up in church are walking away from their faith.[6] Somehow, these young adults seem to have the impression that there's more freedom *outside* the church. But how can that be, since the Bible says, "For freedom Christ has set us free" (Gal. 5:1)? Could we, their controlling moms, be part of the reason the church seems like a house of slavery to them? Could we be creating a dynamic that propels them away from God's family rather than drawing them in? And in doing so, have we threatened their eternal inheritance?

Oh, what a sobering thought.

Friends, we are absolutely called to influence our loved ones. And they are accountable for the way they choose to live their lives. But browbeating our child into meeting *our* expectations does not produce a true child of God. A woman's glaring eyes and coercing tactics can only produce slave-like obedience, not obedience that springs from a willing heart. We must be so careful not to—as Sarah did—unwittingly invite the threat of slavery into our homes.

Here's what this means for me: Rather than lecturing my kids incessantly, I must quietly insist they obey, then hit my knees and pray for God to work in their hearts. Instead of nagging my husband, I must voice my concern, then repeatedly entrust our future to God. Rather than controlling my loved ones by pressuring them into external changes, I must exhort them with truth, then entreat God to work in their hearts.

Sarah couldn't produce a son of Abraham on her own. And I can't produce a son or daughter of God on my own—only God can. Only true sons receive the promised inheritance.

- ❀ What have you, in your own strength, produced that only *mimics* godliness in others? How might this threaten their true faith?

- ❀ List several practical ways you can stop trying to control what only God can do in others' hearts.

- ❀ Read Galatians 5:1. How can you represent God well in your home, based on this verse? Pray, right now, that God would work in the hearts of each of your family members.

For Meditation: Galatians 3:7

By controlling my kids or others, I might produce a pretty convincing imitation Christian, but I can't produce a true son or daughter of God on my own. *God, I will stop trying to control what only you can accomplish in my child's life.*

Sarah's Happy Ending

FOR MOST OF Sarah's life, she agonized over her infertility. She was horribly manipulative, completely obstinate in her pursuit of mom status, and unwilling to consider any viewpoint but her own. But the best part of Sarah's story is that it doesn't end ugly. God intervened, inviting Sarah to give up control and live out her faith, and this is what made her beautiful.

Sarah's Happy Ending inspires any Control Girl with an ugly past to surrender control to the God who brings laughter to life.

Chapter Four

Hagar: Out from Under Her Control

✿ UP UNTIL now, we've seen Hagar's story through Sarah's eyes. But perhaps that's like seeing Cinderella's story through the eyes of the ugly stepsisters. Sarah was the beautiful but entitled rich lady living a life of leisure and ordering her slave girl around. And Hagar was the one saying, "Yes, ma'am," and scurrying to meet Sarah's every demand. Eventually Sarah demanded from Hagar the one thing she couldn't get on her own: an heir.

In her loneliest moment of dejected hopelessness, our Egyptian Cinderella was visited by God himself. He didn't wave a magic wand or fix all of her problems, but he did promise a Happy Ending that exceeded her wildest dreams. So slide the glass slipper on Hagar's foot and consider the story one more time, through her eyes.

Lesson 1: Egyptian Cinderella
Read Genesis 12:10–20; 16:1–4

WHENEVER I WRITE or speak on Control Girls, I'm often asked, *"How do you deal with the controlling person in your life?"* Hagar's story is all about answering that question. More than any other Control Girl we'll study, Hagar was at the mercy of another controlling woman. But ultimately, she was at the mercy of God, who truly *is* in control.

Hagar may have been one of the female servants mentioned in Genesis 12:16, given as a thank-you gift from Pharaoh to Abraham.

Abraham was the rich guy who showed up in Egypt during the famine and gave his beautiful "sister," Sarah, to be Pharaoh's latest wife. Then God struck Pharaoh's household with sickness because of Sarah. Turns out she wasn't Abraham's sister; she was his wife.

Pharaoh got mad and shooed Sarah back to her rightful husband, then kicked the whole clan out, including Hagar. So an Egyptian slave girl found herself in the wilderness caring for a demanding, rich lady who had everything but the one thing she wanted—a baby.

A STATUS UPDATE

There were moments, no doubt, when Hagar looked longingly toward Egypt, the desert wind teasing wisps of dark hair back from her homesick face. Maybe she even entertained thoughts of running away and going home.

Twelve years later, she attempted just that. Hagar's breakout plans were prompted by a new assignment from her mistress: she was to go and sleep with Abraham. Like other slaves of her day, Hagar's body was not her own. She had no rights. She had no choice.

Perhaps Hagar remained detached while her virginity was smothered by the old man she called Master. Maybe she turned her face and let tears trickle silently down her cheek during the sexual act, then stumbled back to her tent.

One thing's for sure: Hagar did not distance herself from the outcome of her new sleeping arrangement. Pregnancy was something she could leverage. And *this* particular pregnancy equaled status.

Hagar's pregnancy catapulted her from a lowly slave position into a position of influence and power. She was Abraham's child-bearer. Her baby was the single heir to the wealth that surrounded her. Rather than looking down on her, now everyone would be looking up. Everyone, including Sarah.

Intoxicated by her new position, Hagar made a dreadful mistake: "When [Hagar] saw that she had conceived, she looked with contempt on her mistress" (Gen. 16:4). Hagar was just trying to survive, but she foolishly allowed arrogance and fresh disdain to seep into her attitude toward Sarah. And Sarah noticed.

CONTROL REVERSALS

There are moments in life when control suddenly tips your way and awakens the dormant Control Girl inside you. Maybe the grandfather, who used to shame and belittle you, is now under your legal guardianship. Or the brother, who made your life miserable as a kid, is now asking for a loan. Maybe you're the one who now has authority. Or a nice figure. Or an upwardly mobile career.

Your response to these teeter-totter shifts in control will tell you something about your heart. Do you immediately capitalize on your elevated status? Do you show contempt and look down your nose? Do you flaunt your new position?

These are trademark moves of a Control Girl.

One day, at age sixteen, I was playing accompaniment for my high school choir. My fingers faltered on the keys, and my rhythm dragged behind the singers. But my choir teacher didn't stop the song to coach me. Rather, he slid onto the piano bench and used his hip to bump me off the end. Without missing a beat, he replaced my flailing fingers with his own sure ones on the keys. I regained my balance and stood awkwardly beside the piano, not sure if I should go sit with the choir or wait until the song ended.

It was an awful moment for me.

I wouldn't want to know how many times I have mentally glared at this scene, fantasizing about boldly marching to the office to report my teacher's rudeness to the principal. The daydream always ends with the teacher either being reprimanded or fired in my presence.

I did nothing at the time, of course. But years later, I realized that there *was* something I could do. I had acquired a new status—I was now an adult. I was also a parent, with a new perspective on the dignity children deserve. And I now served as a youth choir instructor, which I thought gave me the authority to tell this man just how wrong he had been.

And so I did. I wrote him a letter detailing my thoughts on the piano bench experience (among others). I can't remember my exact words, but be assured that as I slid my letter into the mailbox, my chin was tipped *up* as I looked *down* on the man to whom the envelope was addressed.

An Abused Control Girl

My piano bench experience was far from the epitome of abuse. It was a fleeting moment that caused me relatively little pain. Yet look at the mental energy I expended vying to regain my dignity!

How much more urgency is felt by women who truly *have* been abused! Even though slavery is not openly practiced now, there are women all around us who—like Hagar—have been exploited. Their bodies were used to gratify somebody else's appetites. They were violated. There was nothing they could do. And a healthy self-respect demands that they regain control of their dignity.

My friend, if you have been marked by this sort of experience, may I speak softly into your soul? Abuse is horrible. It's wretched. It's *evil*. And I endorse your efforts to hold the one who has mistreated you accountable. Yet I wonder if the resolution you crave will bring the satisfaction you hope for.

Consider Hagar. After control tipped her way, the look of contempt she cast down on Sarah only tossed oil on a flame. The satisfaction of having power over Sarah was a fleeting gratification that invited more abuse, as we're going to see. **What God wants for you is so much richer and deeper and holier than contempt.**

Yes, expressing scorn may gain you some measure of control. It feels *good* to dish out a look of disdain, a shaming letter, or a vengeful attack on the person you were once forced to look *up* to. But lasting satisfaction comes from letting God have control, not taking it yourself (Rom. 12:19).

Now, I'm not proposing passivity. Hear me on this. I'm not suggesting we ignore what happened or cave in to the control tactics of other people. Letting sin rule is never the answer.

What I am suggesting we do is give in to God. Consider the fact that God has witnessed every haunting scene of your life. He saw everything firsthand (Isa. 59:15). He knows about even the exploitation or disrespect you've failed to notice or you've locked out of conscious memory.

And here is what God asks you to do with every abhorrent moment of your life: Let him dish out the consequences. God judges with perfect equity. Psalm 75:7 says, "But it is God who executes judgment, putting down one and lifting up another." God planned to lift Hagar up further than she could have imagined. If only she could have waited on his timing, how much suffering she could have avoided!

When control tips your way, you have a choice. You can leverage your new status, put others down, and get revenge. Or you can let God be in charge.

This won't be quick or easy, especially if you've been abused. Putting God in charge is a process that might take many years, include thousands of baby steps, and require the support of some godly friends. Also, your method for giving God control might differ from someone else's. One woman might press charges. Another might ask for restitution. Still another might drop a dispute altogether. However God directs you, one thing will be consistent: if he's in charge, your face will not be filled with contempt.

Rather than tipping her chin up and dishing out scorn, the woman who hopes in God looks straight into the eye of the one who wronged her and says, "God is the judge. One day you and I will be side by side on bended knee, looking up at God. And he will either sentence you to punishment far more severe than I could ever muster, or he'll pardon you completely, based on the blood of Jesus. In all of this, I defer to him."

❀ Have you ever been the victim of a controlling person? How have you responded?

❀ Are you a Control Girl who has capitalized on a power reversal? How would you respond differently, if you were putting God in control?

❀ Make a list of the wrongs done to you. Now read Psalm 75:2–8. What is one tangible way God wants you to put him in control?

For Meditation: Psalm 9:7–9

God has witnessed every haunting scene of my life firsthand. Rather than dishing out my own scorn, I will put God in control of the consequences. *God, I defer to you as the righteous, just judge.*

Lesson 2: Two Counseling Questions
Read Genesis 16:4–8

RECENTLY, MY HUSBAND and I went on a time-share property tour. We were transparent about our motives and said we were only there to take advantage of the discounted rate at the resort (we're cheap that way). Though we were assured we weren't obligated to buy anything, our sales person took us on as a challenge.

She drew her presentation out, always circling back to the same question—why would we *not* purchase this time-share? She held us hostage for the full two-hour commitment. When Ken encouraged her to continue while I took a call, she folded her arms and said, "No, I'll wait."

After the two-hour mark, I was annoyed. She hadn't even begun the property tour, and I wanted out of there. I started pushing back by giving short, quick answers and reminding her of the time. Then, I demonstrated my speed-walking abilities as we viewed the property, saying, "Uh, huh . . . nice. Can we move on?" My husband was embarrassed by my behavior, but thankful for every second shaved off of that tour. It was a miserable experience, with two Control Girls butting heads.

A FELLOW CONTROL GIRL

Other Control Girls provoke my desire for control. If someone is taking control, I am often *driven* to get it back. This drive is what I see in Hagar.

As a slave, Hagar didn't have many choices. The Bible doesn't reveal her thoughts, so I can't definitively say that Hagar had an I'm-standing-up-on-the-inside attitude. I'm only working off of two clues: her look of contempt, which we previously discussed, and her decision to flee, which we'll consider now. But those are pretty strong clues.

What happened between Sarah and Hagar was nothing less than a battle for control. Once she was carrying Abraham's heir, Hagar prematurely considered herself the victor, but her foolish disdain only caused Sarah to step up her Control Girl game.

Maybe Hagar thought she had already locked in Abraham's loyalty. She *was* having his baby, after all. But when Sarah brought her complaints to Abraham, he refused to get involved. He said, "Behold, your servant is in your power; do to her as you please" (Gen. 16:6).

Hagar must have been shocked and deeply wounded by Abraham's casual dismissal. Two seconds ago, she was gloating. Now, she's being thrown to the first wife, who happens to be baring her teeth and pawing the dirt.

What a devastating situation for Hagar. Without Abraham, she had no shield from the onslaught of Sarah's full-on rage. "Then [Sarah] dealt harshly with [Hagar], and she fled from her" (Gen. 16:6).

The Bible doesn't give details, but here's what we know: Sarah was a bitter, humiliated, emotionally fragile older woman. She was disgraced and angry over the way Hagar insulted her, and she was not held accountable by either a legal system or her husband for how she treated this girl she considered property. Whatever the mistreatment looked like or entailed, it was severe enough that Hagar thought her chances were better in the wilderness.

Many slaves in Hagar's shoes would have lowered their eyes and cowered for as long as necessary under Sarah's rage. We've all heard jaw-dropping stories about people who were locked in basements and beaten for decades, so we know it's possible. But Hagar is not that slave. Rather than cowering, she asserts herself. How? She runs away.

Dashing off into the wilderness, pregnant and alone, is not the mark of a reticent, subservient, downtrodden slave. It's the mark of a Control Girl.

Now Hagar does deserve our sympathy. She has suffered immensely. Her pregnancy and grief are the result of Sarah's selfish insecurity. And Sarah holds all the cards—power, authority, and influence over Abraham. No wonder she's won this battle for control.

Or has she?

Think of Hagar's escape from Sarah's perspective. When Sarah discovered Hagar was missing, do you suppose she said, "Yes, finally, I've won!"? No. People who mistreat others aren't trying to chase them away. What they enjoy is the power they have over a weaker person. To lose control of a victim makes the abuser extremely angry. I picture rage—not relief—on Sarah's face when she learned that Hagar was gone.

So my reasons for claiming Hagar as a fellow Control Girl are her open contempt and assertive response to mistreatment. And though Hagar's reactions seem far more justifiable than my own petty outbursts, I can still learn about God's heart toward me when I study his response to Hagar. Hagar's personal conference with God holds significance for all Control Girls.

GOD'S COUNSELING QUESTIONS

God found Hagar by a wilderness spring. Isn't that the way it always is? We try to take control. We march off independently into the sunset. And then he finds us.

God doesn't begin by lecturing, shaming, or condemning Hagar. He doesn't even share his perspective. Instead, he gently asks her two questions: "Hagar, servant of Sarai, where have you come from and where are you going?" (Gen. 16:8).

God already knows the answers. He did, after all, just call her Hagar, Sarah's servant. God is asking these questions for Hagar's benefit. He's giving Hagar the opportunity to ask *herself*, "What am I trying to escape and what do I want to find?"

The answer to both questions is control.

You don't have to be *in* control to be a Control Girl. Perhaps you're just stomping off to make a statement to some other controlling person. "Stomping off" can include posting a Facebook rant, texting an incriminating photo, ignoring your mom's calls, or filing for divorce.

Wherever you stomp, God goes after you and gently asks the same questions he asked Hagar: "What are you trying to escape and what do you want to find?" Again, the answer to both is control.

Many times, as Control Girls, we haven't thought plainly about that dominating force we're trying to escape, like a controlling father, husband, or church background. Sometimes we fail to recognize that we're running away from some past oppression, like poverty, depression, or addiction.

Where had Hagar come from? Where was she going? God pressed Hagar to look both directions. Was she truly on the path headed to freedom?

Her Ultra-Controlling Mother-in-Law

I recently spoke with a young woman who was intensely irritated by her ultra-controlling mother-in-law. I could almost see her blood pressure rising as she rehearsed all of her mother-in-law's offenses and described her various attempts to free herself from the woman's controlling bondage. She told me she was learning to stand up and take back control, and I had no doubt that was true.

As she talked, I couldn't help but notice her stiff demeanor and angry tone. She sounded entitled and demanding. She sounded, uh . . . *controlling*. It made me wonder if she was truly finding the freedom she longed for. She reminded me of Hagar out on the wilderness path, stomping away from Sarah. Sometimes when we strike out on our own to take back control, we lead ourselves into more bondage, not freedom.

Control Girl, are you stomping off in the opposite direction of some overbearing person or past bondage? If so, won't you stop for a moment and let God come find you? Notice that God didn't come to Hagar while she was traveling in the night or plotting her escape. He waited until she was refreshing herself at a spring, quiet and alone.

Won't you create a quiet moment with God today? Refresh yourself in his presence. Allow his weighty questions to sift down into the depths of your heart. What are you trying to escape? What are you trying to find?

- Which controlling person or situation in your life most gets a rise out of you? How does your reaction reveal your own desire for control?

- Look back at the last two paragraphs of this lesson. Create some quiet time to reflect, ask God for his perspective, and journal your responses.

For Meditation: Galatians 4:8–9

When I try to take back control of my life, I often lead myself into more bondage, not freedom. *God, help me to see with new clarity what I am trying to escape, and what I am trying to gain control of.*

Lesson 3: A Thousand Hurdles
Read Genesis 16:6–16

IN HER LONELIEST moment of hopelessness, our Egyptian Cinderella was visited by God himself. But the scene doesn't go as I'd expect. I want God to come on the scene like a fairy God-the-Father. I want him to wave a wand, dry up her tears, and fix all of her problems. That's what God *does*, right? Not exactly.

This time, he does the opposite. He asks Hagar to go back to the place from which she had just escaped, saying, "Return to your mistress and submit to her" (Gen. 16:9).

I feel a bit disoriented when I hear these words coming from God's mouth. He *knows* what Hagar will be returning to—the slavery, mistreatment, polygamy, and surrogacy! If I'm honest, it makes me wonder what kind of God he is to ask this of her. Going back to Sarah the Horrible? Returning to her second-wife-slave status? To Hagar, the path back must have looked like it was lined with a thousand mountain-sized hurdles.

SHRINKING HURDLES

In middle school, my son had his heart set on running hurdles in track. On the first day of practice, he approached the coach stationed at hurdles and said, "My dad ran hurdles in high school, but I've never tried . . ."

The coach said, "Well, I can tell you right now, you have the wrong build for hurdles." Just then, a kid tripped over a hurdle and landed face-first in the dirt. The coach muttered, "What a little piece of crap."

My son's enthusiasm evaporated instantly. Surely he would fail just like that kid since, apparently, he had the wrong kind of legs. With dashed hopes, he walked away from those hurdles, never to return.

Hope is incredibly powerful. With hope, you can leap over the highest hurdles. Without it, even the smallest one makes you trip.

Friends, God is nothing like my son's track coach. When he turned

Hagar toward the path back, he didn't sneer, criticize, or prophesy that she'd land face-first in a heap. Like a daddy with his hands on the shoulders of a runaway daughter, God gently rotated Hagar toward the path of both surrender and dignity.

Yes, Sarah had been wrong. God acknowledged that, saying, "The LORD has listened to your affliction" (Gen. 16:11). But Hagar was also wrong to run away. God invited this little servant girl to take the honorable path and return, rather than disgracing and endangering herself by playing the fugitive.[1]

Then, like a good coach, God gave Hagar hurdle-shrinking hope. He pointed off into the future, telling Hagar what he planned to do: "I will surely multiply your offspring so that they cannot be numbered for multitude" (Gen. 16:10).

Being mother to a multitude? An exponential family? This was like promising my seventh grader an Olympic gold medal before his first track meet. This was *the* great hope of every woman alive in Hagar's day. Hope of this magnitude would minimize any row of hurdles. And more than just general hope for the future, God gave Hagar specifics.

You don't name the unborn baby of a pregnant girl about to die in the wilderness. But God gave Hagar's baby both a name and a prophecy. Ishmael would be a "wild donkey of a man"—the kind you don't bridle (Gen. 16:12). Oh, what a promise to a runaway slave girl! It meant she would not only live, but one day she and her son would be free.

So Hagar had a choice. Yes, she faced a long row of submission hurdles, but at the end was freedom. Would Hagar welcome the warmth of future blessing, even if it was wrapped for a time in the cloak of slavery?

MINDFUL OF GOD

During the years of the early church, when slavery was still practiced, Peter gave some encouragement to slaves with unjust masters. He said, "For this is a gracious thing, when, mindful of God, one endures sorrows while suffering unjustly" (1 Peter 2:19).

This is consistent with God's encouragement for Hagar. God didn't absolve Sarah or minimize Hagar's suffering. Instead, God asked Hagar to endure Sarah with him in mind. That is, **God asked Hagar to fill her mind with who he is and what he had said.** He asked her to coat her heart with his promises, and then travel the path back to Sarah.

Sometimes, in the face of injustice, God gives his people strength and opportunity to rise up and fight. They rally support, amend governments, and stand up to narcissistic, controlling individuals or widespread corruption. As they shout out their motto, "Correct oppression; bring justice!" (Isa. 1:17), these people represent the very heart of God.

But other times, in the face of struggle and mistreatment, God asks his people to endure. The Bible is filled with examples. Joseph, Daniel, and Esther all were asked to endure mistreatment and hardship. And so are we today.

We live in a morally corrupt world, so all of our lives are tainted with injustice to some degree. And while I would never advise a woman to remain in a situation where she or her children are being harmed, I also would never advise a woman to refuse to endure all mistreatment whatsoever. (I'm not even sure that's possible, unless she secludes herself on a desert island.)

One thing's for sure: God is not naïve or unaware of our mistreatment. One day, his patience will end, and we will see just how intolerant God is of sin. But for now, God sometimes asks us to endure something—at least for a time—that we'd all agree is not right.

He finds us in our desert muttering about the injustice of it all, and like a daddy with his hands on our shoulders, he offers hurdle-shrinking hope. Pointing to the Happy Ending in the distance, God gives us specifics too. There will be streets of gold and no more tears. We'll have justice under Christ's peaceful reign and enjoy pleasures forevermore.

Infused with this hope, God asks us to turn our toes toward uphill surrender. And when a woman "mindful of God . . . endures sorrows while suffering unjustly," God calls her "gracious" (1 Peter 2:19).

A GRACIOUS WOMAN

My friend Dana has endured a troubled marriage for many years. Her husband is emotionally abusive, controlling, and condescending.

He has isolated Dana by telling people she's crazy. He consistently breaks promises and manufactures chaos. He belittles, neglects, blames, and invalidates. Dana's husband is *very* difficult to live with.

At one point, desperate for relief for both herself and her children, Dana filed for divorce. But God blocked her escape and made it clear he wanted Dana to return to her broken marriage—at least for a time. God's call to endure was clear.

Shortly after this, Dana knew her son was in crisis. He asked, "Mom, why did you drop the divorce?" Dana explained that divorce would require her to share him and she wanted to be with him every day. Then she said, "Son, here is my prayer. Every day I ask God to release me from this struggle. Every day. But I don't tell God how to do it. And I don't try to do it alone. I ask God to give me grace for as long as he asks me to stay."

To Dana, the thought of growing old with her husband is overwhelming. Yet the promises she leans on for tomorrow are the same promises that sustained her yesterday. The world, knowing nothing of surrender, might say to Dana, "Why do you put up with this? He's horrible. You deserve more! Why not get the divorce?"

Dana admits that, years ago, she would have been angrily resistant toward anyone suggesting God might direct his child to remain in a situation like hers. But over the years, Dana's perspective has shifted. She says, "I don't see change in my circumstances; I see changes in me. I wouldn't be nearly as dependent on God if life weren't so hard. I see God as very involved, personal, and loving." Dana knows her marriage will still present hurdles. Perhaps thousands of them. But she chooses to be mindful of God, who has told her to stay.

Dana is a dazzling example of someone who "endures sorrows while suffering unjustly." God calls her "gracious," and I agree (1 Peter 2:19). She is kind, thoughtful, and strong—the kind of woman I want to be. She is the complete opposite of a Control Girl.

Has God asked you to stay in a difficult marriage? Or honor a demeaning parent? Has he asked you to press on under a demoralizing boss or a controlling pastor? Do you face hurdles the size of mountains? If so, consider the Happy Ending God has in store for you. Hope of this magnitude can minimize any hurdles. Fill your mind with who he is and what he has said. With your heart coated in hope, turn your toes toward surrender.

   ✿ How does Hagar's story reshape your view of God?

   ✿ If God has asked you to quietly endure an injustice, how can you surrender, not just to this mistreatment but also to God?

   ✿ Picture your Happy Ending as you read Revelation 21:1–7. List any descriptions you find of God and heaven.

For Meditation: 1 Peter 2:18–19

God may ask me to endure sorrows or mistreatment for a time. *God, I will press on by filling my mind with who you are and what you have promised.*

Lesson 4: A Mom at a Distance
Read Genesis 21:8–17

I'M TOLD THAT as a baby, I talked early. Being the firstborn, I called my parents what everyone else called them: Roger and Judie. I would holler from my crib, saying, "Roger . . . Judie . . . Come get me!" Once, after my mom told me no, I needed to lie down and sleep, I began wailing, "Roger, your daughter is *crying!*"

I no longer complain about going to bed. But sometimes, when I face difficulty or suffering, I wail, "God, your daughter is *crying!*" I wonder if he's seeing this situation correctly. The Control Girl in me wants to let him know. And the little girl inside needs to know if he even cares.

Back when Hagar was a fugitive in the desert, pregnant with Ishmael and running from Sarah's mistreatment, she named God, the "God of seeing" (Gen. 16:13). Sixteen years later, back in the wilderness, Hagar must have asked herself, "Is he seeing *this?*"

This time, she wasn't sneaking away in the night. She was being evicted, under the bright morning sun, and sent away with only a loaf of bread and a canteen of water. And who's the one turning her out? It's Abraham, the father of her teenage son. Yes, it's true that Ishmael teased Sarah's little boy at the party. But was that enough reason to cast them out?

Abraham put the meager supplies on Hagar's shoulders, not even sparing a mule for his firstborn son and second wife. It was a death sentence for both of them, and Hagar knew it.

If there's anything a Control Girl mom wants for her child, it's a secure future. She invests heavily and is willing to do whatever it takes to create the Happy Ending she has in mind for him, whether that means advocating for him, fighting off bullies, or eliminating threats.

But what if, backed into a corner, a mom doesn't have what it takes to fight for that Happy Ending? Well, that's a desperate place for a Control Girl mom. And it's the exact place in which Hagar found herself.

The food and water were gone. Hagar had no way to keep her son alive. This was totally out of her control, and she was devastated.

A Mom Who Abandons

Once the water runs out, the narrator of Genesis 21:15–16 goes to a lot of trouble to describe how Hagar positions her son and herself:

- She "put" the child under one of the bushes (we'll come back to this word).
- Then she went and sat down opposite him, a good way off (facing him, but at a distance).
- He was about the distance of a bowshot away (so still in her sight).
- And she lifted up her voice and wept.

Desperate mothers often can't be dragged from the bedside of their dying children, yet Hagar "puts" her dying boy beneath a bush and walks away. If this makes you shudder, just wait. The word translated "put" means she "cast" or "flung" him beneath the bush, and has a connotation of abandonment![2] What is Hagar doing here?

Psalm 55:22 clarifies. The same Hebrew word used here is translated as "cast": "Cast your burden on the LORD, and he will sustain you." Later, this psalm is echoed in 1 Peter 5:7: "Casting all your anxieties on him, because he cares for you."

So when Hagar casts her teenage son beneath the bush and abandons him there, she is anything but calloused or detached. Her physical action represents something very significant. By casting her son from her arms, Hagar is thrusting him into God's. She's relinquishing control.[3]

A good mom does what Hagar did. She helps her child as much as she can, and then she abandons him to God. She leaves her child on the altar and backs away, giving God full control over what happens next. But she doesn't do it easily.

Surrendering to the living God a child that you have held, cared for, and loved from birth is deeply costly. It's fitting that Hagar lifted up her voice and wept. I imagine it wasn't a quiet whimper, but rather the sort of crying that involves sobbing and choking in snotty desperation.

"God Hears"

How does God respond when Hagar "puts" her boy beneath that bush? Does he notice, show interest, and respond? Yes! Perhaps, foreseeing the future as he does, God had this very moment in mind when he said, "You shall call his name Ishmael" (Gen. 16:11). For Ishmael means "God hears."

Here is a boy without an inheritance, without a father, without food or water, and even without the comfort of a mother nearby. Yet he was not without a God who hears.

When you're dying of dehydration with parched, cracked lips, you can't even produce tears, let alone screams. Your hoarse cries are no louder than a whisper. Yet they are loud enough for the Lord.

God's messenger told Hagar, "God has heard the voice of the boy where he is" (Gen. 21:17). I love that last little tag "where he is." Because, where is Ishmael? He's a bowshot away.

This is the position in which many a mom finds herself, especially if she's done the hard work of relinquishing control to God. She looks on, but at a distance. She wishes she could hold her baby snugly and rock him in her arms, but those days are gone. The distance has crept in, and she has no way to soothe, comfort, or help.

At a Distance

Brenda grieves deeply over the way her daughter, Savanah, has removed herself from their family. It started with a controlling college boyfriend, and then escalated to private wedding plans and severed communication with all family and friends. To learn the date of Savanah's wedding, Brenda and her husband had to look on a gift registry website.

Since their family was always close, this was devastating. On Mother's Day, aching to be close to her daughter, Brenda, her husband, and their kids quietly formed a prayer circle out in front of Savanah's apartment. Soon the police came, responding to complaints that they were "disturbing the peace." Brenda had to drive away in anguish and abandon her daughter to the big, wise hands of God.

The pain of watching from a distance as your child suffers on the brink of disaster is almost intolerable. But Hagar's story shows that even when we are far from our beloved children, God is not. From the time you can cup your baby in your hands till the day she drives off into the sunset, she is safely tucked into God's good hands. She's been there since before she was born.

Does God hear his daughter crying? Does he hear his daughter's *child* crying? Yes, he does. And he cares deeply.

❀   List the threats to your child's well-being today. Write Psalm 55:22 above this list.

❀   Write out any tangible ways God wants you to cast your burdens into his hands. How does it help to know he cares?

❀   Are you agonizing from a distance while your child (or another loved one) struggles? Write a prayer, trusting God to lean in close, even when you can't.

For Meditation: 1 Peter 5:7

Even when I agonize at a distance while my child suffers on the brink of disaster, God is leaning close, hearing my child's parched cry. *Lord, I surrender and even abandon my child to you.*

Lesson 5: Opened Eyes
Read Genesis 21:16–21

HAVE YOU EVER been powerless to save your child? That's a silly question, really, because all of us are powerless to save our children from tragedy all of the time. Yet have you ever been made acutely aware of the fact?

For Angela, it was when her daughter, Shelby, had whooping cough at age five. On four different occasions, they called an ambulance because Shelby had stopped breathing and was turning blue. Angela remembers screaming to her husband, "Kevin, *do* something!" and then crying out in desperation, "Breathe for her, Jesus!"

Each time, the ambulance would have been too late. But each time, God brought Shelby back from the brink of death and delivered her into the frantic arms of her parents who had been unable to *do* anything to save her.

GOD'S PLAN

In lesson 4, we watched Hagar back away from her boy, powerless to save him. Perhaps she had once been a pushy, hovering, controlling mom, but not now. There in the wilderness, she was out of ideas. She had no strength or resources. Her plans had expired, and she was desperate.

God had been in control all along, calmly providing for Ishmael and protecting him. But now, God gives Hagar a role. He says, "Up! Lift up the boy, and hold him fast with your hand, for I will make him into a great nation" (Gen. 21:18). After Hagar was out of ideas, God invited her to support his plans.

I often do this backward and invite God to support *my* plans. As the mom, I feel that I somehow have jurisdiction over these emerging little people and their futures. My plans have been in the making for *years*. I only call upon God when we hit a bump in the road and need support. I say, "Up! Lift up my daughter and make her popular, so she can have great influence for you." Or, "Up! Help my son make the soccer team so his confidence will grow, and he'll become a risk-taker for you."

But God doesn't jump up and join my plans. He says it should be the other way around. **Instead of inviting him to support *my* plan, God calmly remains on his throne and invites *me* to support *his* plan.**

God's plan for my child is more detailed, elaborate, and long-term than mine. He has thought deeper, and his perspective spans wider. His plan began before I even realized I was pregnant. He created my child for his purposes, which are far greater than mine and will continue after I'm gone. God often waits until I'm out of ideas to say, "Up! Lift him up and take him by the hand, for I am going to do something great with his life."

And when I jump up, not as the pushy, hovering, controlling mom, but as the humble mom, completely desperate for God's direction, that's when God opens my eyes. That is what he did for Hagar.

"Then God opened her eyes, and she saw a well of water. And she went and filled the skin with water and gave the boy a drink" (Gen. 21:19).

GOD OPENED HER EYES

Imagine Hagar's teary, wonder-filled eyes as she caught her first glimpse of the nearby well. Imagine the intense, joyful worship on her face as she bolted to fill the flask! How the water must have sloshed over the edges as she hastily rushed it back to the cracked lips of her precious son.

He drank.

He lived.

He became an expert with the bow and grew up to be the father of twelve sons— Hagar's grandsons. Ishmael's whole story hinged on a well that had been there all along, hidden from Hagar until God "opened her eyes."

Why does God sometimes hide a solution and keep me from seeing it? God wants me to stop trusting in myself for solutions to my kids' problems. He cares even more deeply for my children than I do. He wants to be the one to provide for them and has all sorts of creative ways to do so. He stands by, ready to open eyes, unlatch gates, and release resources.

He's just waiting for me to despair of my own solutions, and cry out—in faith—to him.

God could have kept little Shelby breathing steadily, free of whooping cough. He could have caused Hagar to readily see the well. But sometimes God waits. He conceals the solution. And he presses desperate mothers to turn their eyes to him.

❁ What situation pressed you to recognize that you cannot fix every problem your child (or loved one) faces?

❁ How has God opened your eyes to a solution that you didn't see before? How did this help you see that God is providing, and not you?

❁ Write out your ideal plans for your children. Now burn or shred these plans and praise God that his plans are so much wiser and far-reaching. Read Jeremiah 29:11 aloud, inserting your child's name.

For Meditation: Psalm 22:9–11

God has all sorts of creative ways to care for my loved ones. Rather than trusting in myself to find solutions, God wants me to cry out to him. *God, I believe that you can open my eyes to provisions that are hidden from me.*

Hagar's Happy Ending

WE BEGAN BY casting Hagar as our Egyptian Cinderella. And though a Prince Charming never showed up, Hagar's encounter with the "God Who Sees" put into motion a Happy Ending more enchanting than her wildest dreams.

Though Hagar didn't realize it at first, being kicked out by Sarah was God's way of keeping his promise. He was escorting her to freedom! Just as God would one day do for Israel, he released Hagar from slavery, sent her into the wilderness, and cared for her every need.

There in the wilderness, with nothing but a dry flask, Hagar crossed the threshold into the rich, free life she always longed for. Ishmael became an expert archer, married an Egyptian girl, and had twelve sons—each a prince over his own tribe (Gen. 21:21; 25:16).

God doesn't always release his people immediately. Sometimes he leaves us tangled up in complicated situations like Hagar's for what seems like an eternity. But God always has a Happy Ending in store for those who surrender to him.

Chapter Five

Rebekah: Standing In for God

🌼 REBEKAH'S STORY opens like an unfurling rose: Once upon a time, in a faraway land, there lived a beautiful maiden named Rebekah. The young girl was visited by a butler, who had traveled a great distance to find her. He whisked Rebekah into the arms of her love-at-first-sight prince, and they were married immediately. Before long, while they were expecting their first child, a prophecy was given about their unborn child's fate . . .

You almost have to pinch yourself as a reminder that this is all true. With a beginning like that, Rebekah's story is sure to have a Happy Ending, right? But Control Girls have a way of disrupting the story line.

Lesson 1: God Threads the Knot
Read Genesis 24

WHEN I WAS twenty-three, I moved to Milwaukee. I had exactly two friends there: Chris and Jamie Brauns. They brought dinner over the day I moved in and, as we ate, Chris shared a story from his day.

Chris was a Christian education pastor and had received a call informing him that the fourth grade boys' teacher had quit. But after the call ended, immediately the phone rang again. This time it was Ken Popkin calling to say, "I'd like to teach Sunday school. Maybe fourth grade boys?" Chris said he just happened to have an opening.

We all laughed about the providential timing of the calls. Then my new roommate, who also went to the church, mentioned, "I know Ken Popkin from the singles group. He's really good-looking."

As I lay in bed that night recalling the events of the day, I whispered into the darkness, "Well, at least there's *one* good-looking single guy in Milwaukee. And if he's willing to teach fourth-grade boys, he's *got* to be a good guy!"

I think God was listening to my thoughts with a big grin on his face that night. Because two years later, I wore my white dress and walked down the aisle into the arms of the Sunday school teacher of my dreams. (And yes, he is quite handsome.)

My heart swells every time I consider all the details God arranged to create that bit of foreshadowing. He prompted the back-to-back phone calls on that very day, arranged the dinner guests, and inspired the conversation—all as a teaser for the new girl in town.

REBEKAH'S LOVE STORY

Our God loves stirring up a good love story. And if ever a love story was providential, it was Rebekah's. One ordinary evening, at the spring near her house, a traveling stranger asked her for a drink. Rebekah lowered her water jar for him, and then also offered to water his ten camels. Since a single camel can drink about twenty-five gallons, it took her many sweaty trips between the spring and the trough—while the man eerily watched her.

When she finished, he surprised her with gold bracelets and a gold nose ring. He asked whose daughter she was and if there was room for his entourage to stay overnight. When Rebekah graciously offered the hospitality of her father, the son of Nahor, the man did something even more unusual. He bowed to worship God. He said that God had led him directly to the relatives of his master (Gen. 24:27)!

So this man was the servant of a relative? What a coincidence. Rebekah ran home to tell her family. Her brother, seeing the jewelry, ran to urge the man inside. Once inside, the man insisted on immediately telling his story.

He began by unveiling his identity: He was the servant of Abraham—the long-lost brother of Nahor (Rebekah's grandfather). While away, God had blessed Abraham with great wealth and, at age one hundred, Sarah had borne him a son. Isaac was to inherit everything, and Abraham was adamantly against him marrying one of the local girls who might turn his heart from God. So Abraham asked the servant to fetch a bride from among the distant relatives.

At first the servant was skeptical. "Perhaps the woman will not follow me," he said (v. 39). But Abraham had assured him that, with God's guidance, he would find the right girl.

So after a five-hundred-mile trip, here he was. And at the spring he had prayed for God's direction—specifically, that the right girl would offer to water his ten camels. Then, before he finished the prayer, Rebekah had appeared with her water jar.

Surely Rebekah's eyes widened at this point in the story. A man had prayed a prayer involving a girl watering camels, and she had unknowingly stepped forward to do just that? Also, she *happened* to be unwed and of the exact family he was seeking?

We love stories of providence like these, where God arranges the details of a five-hundred-mile journey so that the servant shows up at the exact time and place in which the girl is about to appear. Stories of providence cause our hearts to swell with wonder. We throw our heads back and say, "Yes! God, you are in control."

Will You Go?

The follow-up to providence is more difficult. No matter how sweet the story line, there's always sacrifice required. This was certainly the case with Rebekah.

I have a sixteen-year-old daughter. She's lovely, gracious, kind, and hardworking, and someday she will be a prize for some lucky fella. But today, if she brings a long-lost relative home for dinner, and if he tells a fantastical story of how she served him the moment he prayed . . . I might think it was a neat story. But I would not pack her up like a mail-order bride.

I know things were different back then, but certainly parents still agonized over having their daughters whisked across the country. Certainly teenage girls grieved the costliness of leaving behind everything familiar and dear.

Understandably, Rebekah's parents struggled. They couldn't deny God's providential hand, but they objected to the servant's idea of leaving immediately. So they let Rebekah decide. "Will you go with this man?" they asked (Gen. 24:58).

She could have sulked, scowled, trembled, or howled. (We'll see later that Rebekah was capable of such antics.) Yet her response was unscripted and beautiful.

"I will go," she said.

Providence doesn't exempt us from surrender. God may bring 437 details together, but ultimately we have to choose. *Will you go?* the Lord asks. *Will you step out in faith? Will you entrust your future into my hands?*

My love story was consequential to taking a position in Milwaukee— my biggest faith-step yet at age twenty-three. After an interview, I stayed the weekend and visited Chris and Jamie's church. Single girl that I was, I discreetly scanned the pews for interesting young men.

Zilch. I didn't see even *one* hopeful dating candidate. (I'm sure several guys were missing that day.) This was quite a contrast from back home, where my church seemed to be teeming with handsome, godly single men. Since my primary objective in life at that point was to figure out my last name, the thought of not sharing the same zip code with masses of marriage potentials seemed risky, like I wasn't playing the odds very well.

But God often asks us to exhibit extreme faith by doing something *against* the odds. My march into Milwaukee may not have seemed like a parade to anybody else, but in my heart, I was raising a banner that declared, "God, you're in control!"

By giving up control, I *invited* God's providence. Rebekah clearly did the same. Why else would a young girl discard all of the hopes and plans she had cherished up until yesterday? Why would she leave home and move cross-country to marry a stranger? Rather than imagining a dreadful fate, Rebekah relished God's sovereignty over the details of her life, including a trip to the well and a traveling stranger.

God is in control. His fingers are strong enough for the intricate detail work. He is near, involved, and powerful. He will have his way. **But God gets the most glory not when he rips control from our hands but when we invite him, open-palmed, to have his way with us.** When our eyes widen at the glimpse of his foreshadowing and our warm, pliable hearts invite his providence, he is pleased. When we say, "I will go," he smiles.

- Which providential details in your life cause your heart to swell, knowing that God was in control and cared enough to bring them together?

- How has God's providence created pain or cost for you? How does revisiting the providential details from your past help you surrender the cost?

For Meditation: Proverbs 16:33

God gets the most glory, not when he rips control from my hands, but when I warmly invite him to take it. *God, thank you for your strong fingers, which providentially shape the details that form my life.*

Lesson 2: When One Walks Away
Read Genesis 25:19–26; Romans 9:6–23

I RECENTLY ASKED my kids if they have any childhood memories of me being a Control Girl. All three of them brought up a particular event involving a candle. They remember it like this: I was talking about salvation, and rather than somberly listening, four-year-old Cade was being silly. So I turned off the lights, lit a candle, and made Cade hold his hand over the flame until it got uncomfortably hot. I talked forcefully about hell, with all of its outer darkness and endless flames. The resulting impression I made was probably not what I intended . . . my kids thought I was crazy!

Though I don't remember the candle episode, I have no trouble identifying what would motivate me to do such a thing. Nothing terrifies me more than the possibility of my children rejecting God. If the path to destruction is wide, then I will use whatever I can—including open flames—to motivate my kids toward the narrow path leading to life (Matt. 7:13).

I would absolutely love to get my Control Girl hands on the Book of Life and personally inscribe their names in permanent ink (Rev. 20:15). But Rebekah's story reminds me that **my child's destiny is held in God's wise, capable hands, not my faltering, grabby ones**.

TWINS

Like Sarah, Rebekah struggled with infertility. But after twenty years, Isaac's prayers were answered. Rebekah conceived.

When Rebekah became alarmed by the violent jostling in her womb, she asked God what was going on. He gave her both an ultrasound snapshot and a glimpse into the future. Her womb held *two* babies, actually, and these baby boys were trying to smash each other. Their fight over limited space was indicative of the days to come, when they would battle it out over boundary lines.

> Two nations are in your womb,
>> and two peoples from within you shall be divided;
> the one shall be stronger than the other,
>> the older shall serve the younger. (Gen. 25:23)

If this had just been a prophecy about twins, Rebekah would have been elated. Twins would double the progress of her family becoming—per God's promise—as numerous as the stars. But Rebekah's prophecy also predicted a disturbing family division. Her twin boys wouldn't become one nation *together*; they would be a house divided.

This went completely against the common practices of Rebekah's day. Back then, when a patriarch died, his land wasn't divided equally among his sons. Rather, the lion's share went to the oldest, who became the head of the clan and a benefactor for all.[1] This kept them together, working collectively for the family's success.

Just as surely as I envision my able-bodied adult sons *not* living together on my land, Rebekah expected the opposite. So God's words struck like a shocking thunderbolt. Eventually Rebekah's family tree did split into two nations, just like God said. The younger twin, Jacob, became the father of Israel, God's people. And Esau became the father of the Edomites, enemies to God's people.

One twin was a follower of God; the other wasn't.

GOD'S CONTROL

Romans 9, which is all about God's chosen people, retells the story of Rebekah's twins. While the twins were still jostling about in Rebekah's womb, God chose Jacob, the younger brother, to be the father of his people. God's choice, the text points out, was not based on anything the boys did or didn't do. They weren't even born yet.

This kicks up a whole lot of salvation questions, all pointing to the fact that the twins were still inside Rebekah's womb when God singled out one branch of the family tree to bless. We wonder about the people we love. Has God singled *them* out to bless too?

While this story emphasizes God's sovereignty, it would be a mistake to conclude that we should be passive toward God, or that we have no choice over our destiny. Esau, the older twin, had choices. And his choices repeatedly led him away from God. First, he willingly gave up his birthright, and then he married Canaanite women.

We all make our own choices, as do the people we love. Any person can turn toward God and be blessed. Jesus says, "Whoever comes to me I will never cast out" (John 6:37). Because of this, whenever I talk to my children about the gospel, I put plenty of emphasis—as the Bible does—on their responsibility to turn from sin and come to Jesus for salvation.

A COMFORTING TRUTH

But what if one of my children *doesn't* choose to follow God? The possibility of our destinies being split, like Rebekah's family tree, is devastating. I want every single one of my children—along with the rest of the people I love—to turn toward God and be saved. Does God have control over this? Or is my loved one responsible for turning to him?

The answer to both is *yes*. This seeming contradiction can't be boiled down into something simple and transparent. Theologians have been challenging each other over this for centuries, and I would be presumptuous to think I have anything to add to the conversation.

But I'd like to single out one facet of truth from Rebekah's story that I believe is incredibly helpful for Control Girls. Here it is: salvation is not based on who your mom is (the twins had the same mother), nor is it based on what you do or don't do to earn God's favor (the twins hadn't done anything yet).

This is actually quite comforting. What if the responsibility for my kids' salvation *did* fall on me? What if it was my job to corral them onto the narrow path? What if their eternity hinged on my ability to get them to earn God's approval? How terrifying and exhausting! I can only imagine what sort of candle-burning mother I'd become. My life would be one big, frantic fit of prodding, pressing, and urging my children toward God. And if one brazenly turned *away* from God? Oh, just think of the controlling monster-mama I'd become.

And what would all of this say about God? If I *were* able to procure

God's approval, he wouldn't be in control; I would be. And would *that* be comforting? Not at all! I find far more reassurance knowing that my kids' salvation is not based on their efforts to win God's approval or *my* efforts to get them moving in the right direction.

PRODIGAL SON

Mary Katherine never expected her son to turn from God. As a boy, Peter had been so spiritually insightful. At age two, he told her, "I am a sinner, and I need the saving grace of Jesus." Mary Katherine figured he was the next Billy Graham, and everybody at church agreed. Nobody thought Peter would become a prodigal.

But when Peter was fifteen, Sunday mornings turned into stressful power struggles: he refused to attend church, and Mary Katherine threatened to ground him for a month. Peter's rebellion mushroomed, and Mary Katherine felt increasingly responsible. Certainly this was a reflection of her parenting. Perhaps she hadn't gotten the formula right. She needed to do more! So she clamped down harder on Peter, hounding him with Scripture and warnings.

It became a vicious cycle with Mary Katherine trying to get control and Peter pulling further away. He turned to drug and alcohol abuse and domestic violence, and got acquainted with the local jail.

One day, as she was journaling, God showed Mary Katherine something new. She had tried to create an ideal childhood environment for Peter, allowing only Christian friends, movies, and music. But God reminded Mary Katherine that even in a perfect environment with a perfect Parent, Adam and Eve rebelled. So why would she assume that in a broken environment, with a broken parent, her son would *not* rebel?

From that day forward, God began prying back Mary Katherine's controlling fingers. Then one day, via Facebook, Peter threatened to kill himself. *I can't control that*, Mary Katherine thought. And for the first time, she felt completely relieved of the burden she had carried for so long. She was not responsible for Peter's salvation. *God* was the one who could save him. Not her.

Today, Mary Katherine prays desperately for her son, longing for him to turn back to God. She can't control how long or how far he wanders. But Mary Katherine finds comfort from knowing this is *not* in her hands; it's in God's.

The violent jostling in Rebekah's belly is good imagery for the life struggle that each of my children face. Will they turn toward or against God? Mercifully, God refuses to let me answer that. He invites me to put out my candles and, like Mary Katherine, surrender even this over to him.

✿   Salvation is God's work. Have you made it your own? List any evidence you see, such as anxiety, pressuring, fretting, or angry reactions to a child's rebellion.

✿   Pray for each unrepentant prodigal whom you know and love, and rest your hope for their salvation on God alone, knowing that he is the one who saved you (Ps. 42:5).

For Meditation: Romans 9:16

My child's salvation is in God's wise, capable hands, not my faltering, grabby ones. How terrifying it would be if I *were* in control. *Father, I find comfort in knowing that you are in control of my child's destiny, not me.*

Lesson 3: Differences Can Be Wedges or Fasteners
Read Genesis 25:27–34

DURING MY YOUNGEST son's childhood, I seemed to constantly have him on my hip, rushing from one activity to the next. Sometimes, en route, he would tug my chin and say, "Mommy, yook me." He wanted to draw my attention away from whatever his siblings were doing. He wanted me to see him, and really hear what he was saying. He wanted my face to light up at his ideas. He wanted my attention and approval, just like the big kids.

Sometimes, I was careful to give each of my kids the individual affirmation they craved, saying, "Good job, honey. Wow!" Other times, usually when I was trying to get control, I did the opposite. I withheld my approval and said, "Look at sissy. Why can't you listen like her?"

Thankfully I didn't do this constantly. Comparison may be a great way to control your kids, but it drives wedges between them that far outlast any momentary gains. Sibling rivalry is natural, but our parenting can either heal the friction between our children or contribute to it.

HIS AND HERS

Rebekah's twin boys were as different as they could be. But Genesis 25:28 shines a huge flashlight on a bigger cause for tension: "Isaac loved Esau because he ate of his game, but Rebekah loved Jacob."

Naming your favorite twin couldn't have been marriage-enhancing. And it certainly wasn't helpful for the twins. When family conflict began to escalate, Genesis 27 records each parent beckoning their twin of choice. Isaac called Esau (v. 1) and Rebekah called Jacob (v. 6). Their "his and hers" parenting only drove deeper the wedge between two very dissimilar brothers.

Family dynamics dramatically affect who we are. That's why, before a counselor can help someone, he tries to gain insight into the person's background with questions like, "How would you describe your parents?

What did your family value most? Tell me about your siblings. What significant childhood events stand out?"

If Jacob had gone to counseling, here's how he might have responded:

My twin brother and I are complete opposites. He has lots of red hair and the temper to go with it. I'm more contemplative and cultured. As kids, Esau was always outside hunting with Dad, and I liked being inside with Mom. There was this one day when Esau came in from hunting, famished. I offered to trade him my homemade soup for his birthright. He shrugged and said, "What good's a birthright if I starve?" That's how little it meant to him.

Apparently, Esau was born with my hand grabbing his heel, as if I was trying to keep him from beating me. I think I still resent that he won, especially because of how dismissive he is of our family heritage.

God chose our family to be his people. We take our faith very seriously. We circumcise our males as a sign of our covenant with God. We worship him only, which means we separate ourselves from the Canaanites. My grandfather even sent a servant hundreds of miles to fetch Mom to be Dad's bride. That's how important it is for us not to marry the Canaanites.

But guess what Esau did. He married two Canaanite wives. My mom was heartbroken. Esau's wives make her life bitter, and she's devastated to see her grandkids picking up godless Canaanite habits. But Esau just shrugs and does whatever he feels like.

My dad, though, is so fond of Esau. It drives me insane. He likes the game Esau hunts, which is such a stupid, small reason to approve of him.

I'm Mom's favorite. Everyone knows it. She's grateful I haven't caved and married a Canaanite. I'm resolved, like her. She left her whole family to come as a foreigner and be a part of God's chosen family—that's how strong she is.

So, we're kind of a house divided—Dad and Esau versus Mom and me.

NIGHT AND DAY FAMILY

Like with Jacob's family, God seems to make a habit of piecing together families of individuals who *aren't* alike. Surely it's his idea to make "opposites attract" and marry each other. And he often pairs contrasting siblings, like Cain and Abel or Jacob and Esau.

Another example of God mixing sharp contrast into the DNA of a family is my own. My husband and I are extreme opposites, and our kids are all very distinct and unique. But **God intends for my family's differences to serve as fasteners, not wedges**.

Whenever the Bible talks about God's family, it emphasizes our differences. We're compared to a body, where each unique member both contributes to the whole and depends on the others (1 Cor. 12:25). God designed our differences to *unite* us, not create sibling rivalry.

And God doesn't play favorites. He never says, "Why can't you be like your sister?" His favor is never based on how we compare to someone else. In fact, it's not based on behavior at all. Each of us is loved unconditionally, and our differences are *embraced*, rather than tolerated or scorned.

First Corinthians 12:18 says that God meticulously arranged the members of the body of Christ. And this is true not just for the church but for our families as well. Think of your family as a micro church, fastened together by God. Each person is strategically placed in your family for the good of the whole. Romans 12:5 says, "Each one of us is joined with one another, and we become together what we could not be alone" (VOICE).

Suppose Jacob and Esau had grown up in a home like this, where differences united instead of divided. What if Esau had learned to depend on Jacob's levelheadedness, and Jacob relied on Esau's passion? What if their mom had trained them to support each other, rather than capitalize on moments of weakness?

Oh, the damage we do when we try to prune away others' differences, based on our own preferences. God designed us to be unique, not uniform. When Control Girl moms use sibling comparisons to get control, we shove wedges between our kids. And favoritism is like an axe down the middle of the family tree. Let's parent the way God parents us. Let's celebrate others' differences the way God—the Creator of individuality—does! He designed our differences to be the fasteners that bind us together as spiritual siblings, so that together we become what we could never be on our own.

- Which person(s) have you most tried to change?
- How have you used comparison to try to gain control? Confess your sin, both to God (the Creator of individuality) and to the one(s) you've offended.
- Read Romans 12:4–8 and list the spiritual gifts and character qualities that each person in your family contributes to the good of the whole.

For Meditation: Romans 12:5

We are all different by God's design. Those differences are intended to be fasteners, not wedges, in the family of God. *God, I will celebrate others' differences, instead of trying to control them.*

Lesson 4: Four Ways to Repent of Control
Read Genesis 27

THE TANTALIZING THING about control is that it seems so promising. We're just sure that if we could finagle a few trend-setting details, we'll set things in motion to secure the Happy Ending we're so desperate to have. *How* we get control seems irrelevant, compared to locking in on the last page.

Often, when it's too late to turn back, we have the sickening realization that those earlier pages were more important than we thought. Our resentful, insulting, scandalous behavior *did* have an impact. All of those controlling maneuvers added up to something. Ironically, miserable consequences are often the result of trying to make everything turn out right.

Control Girl tales don't lead to Happy Endings. They begin with a woman trying to bulldoze her way to happiness, and end with heaps of relational rubble. Rebekah's story is no exception.

Let's take apart the ways Rebekah both finagled control and sabotaged her family relationships. But as we do, let's also heed the warning from God that's tucked into this story. How we treat our family can make rubble of our own relationships. What are some specific control habits we can repent of before it's too late? Rebekah's story provides four: eavesdropping, pitting people against each other, being deceitful, and ignoring risk.

EAVESDROPPING

As Isaac made secret plans to bless Esau, not Jacob, Rebekah was listening at the door. Rebekah, who was vehemently opposed to this plan, could have walked in and said, "Isaac, can we talk about this?" But instead, she chose to use the illicit information to plan her countermove.

Eavesdropping is commonplace for Control Girls.

- A mom digs through her daughter's diary, looking for dating relationship information.

· A wife adds spyware to her husband's phone, trying to catch him with another woman.
· A woman hacks into her coworker's email, looking for correspondence about herself.
· A mother-in-law reads the texts on her daughter-in-law's unlocked phone.

Controlling women are quick to disrespect privacy lines to gather hidden information. Not knowing means having no control. But when we pry into concealed information, we drain trust from our relationships.

How to repent: Give up eavesdropping. This includes listening in on, thumbing through, hacking into, and fishing around. Yes, you have concerns. Every woman does. But rather than extracting private information, turn to the Lord. Wait on him to prompt the deep conversations that need to happen, or unveil the issues that need to be addressed.

Your loved one may very well be doing things you don't approve of. But God—who sees perfectly in the dark—can hold her or him accountable far more effectively than you can by picking through the trash.

Let me add a qualifying word to protective moms, like me. As babies, our kids have no privacy and it doesn't bother them one bit. As they grow, this changes. It's natural for them to want independence and privacy, but this should be a gradual process. Just because my child now gets dressed behind closed doors doesn't mean he's ready to handle Facebook, texting, and Snapchat with no supervision. The younger the child, the more vulnerable he is. But as our kids inch toward adulthood, we moms must constantly gauge whether we are motivated by protectiveness or a desire for control.

PITTING PEOPLE AGAINST EACH OTHER

Stop and consider. Why did Rebekah fly to her favorite son to repeat what she overheard? I'll give you a hint: it wasn't out of protective compassion for her son.

Rebekah knew that it would stir up all sorts of emotions in Jacob to learn that his father planned to bless Esau and not him. But she was focused on recruiting him for her countermove, not preserving relationships. Once she saw steam coming out of Jacob's ears, Rebekah said, "Don't worry, I have a plan. We'll trick your dad into blessing you instead." This is not a caring mother giving carefully measured advice to her son. This is an angry, outmaneuvered Control Girl enlisting her son's help to strike back. Rebekah's plan is the equivalent of throwing a grenade at the family tree. It's a face-off for control that will not end well.

Control Girls are masterminds at pitting people against each other. We intuitively know how to share inflammatory information in a way that will solicit support for our control-gathering vendettas. We say things like, "Did you know your father is seeing someone new?" Or, "I wanted you to know what he said about you." Or, "Since your kids are affected by this, I thought you should know."

How to repent: Stop sharing information that will divide people. Proverbs 16:28 says, "A whisperer separates close friends." A woman with a pure, untwisted heart works to fortify relationships, not damage them. She repeats the good things people say about each other. She endears them to each other. She sows seeds of peace, not discord.

Sure, she still sees the unfair treatment, betrayal, and rudeness. But for the sake of relationships, she refrains from passing out grenades. Rather than using conflict to her advantage or to solicit support for her side, the woman who relinquishes control to God keeps the circle small while working through hurtful disagreements.

BEING DECEITFUL

Backstage, Rebekah disguised Jacob as Esau. She put him in a hairy goatskin costume with an outdoor smell. Then she put the prop in his hand—a meal that mimicked Esau's house special. It would be a benefit performance, with Rebekah and Jacob benefiting. But Rebekah's deceitful tactics were not authorized by God and served only to rupture her already fragile relationships.

Imagine Jacob's pain. He got to hear the blessing he longed for, but it was meant for his brother, not him. This didn't feel like receiving a blessing; it felt like a betraying curse. And imagine Isaac's pain, after realizing his wife had exploited his blindness. What a deplorable way for a wife to treat her husband. Her brazen disrespect is sickening.

Ongoing deception is like a lit stick of dynamite under a marriage. A Control Girl can masterfully dress things up to please her husband. But if, behind that warm meal, clean house, tidy budget, and intimate evening, is a deceitful woman only "performing" to conceal her agenda, her marriage is at risk of blowing up. And by inviting the kids to join the act, she only amplifies the threat. Disguising, sneaking, and hiding are great ways to get control. However, **deception and relational intimacy are mutually exclusive. You can't have both.**

How to repent: Be honest. Be completely open with your husband or others about your motives. Ask for what you want honestly, and be willing to accept a *no*. That's part of giving up control.

If you've been wearing a mask for a while, it can be painful to lower it. But when you unselfishly love someone, you won't continue deceiving them.

Make yourself vulnerable. Confess your deception. Strengthen and renew the relationship by honoring the other person with your integrity. Romans 12:9-10 says, "Let love be genuine. . . . Love one another with brotherly affection. Outdo one another in showing honor."

Ignoring Risk

Jacob initially rejected his mom's plan. He said, "Dad might discover I'm not Esau! He might curse me instead of bless me." But Rebekah assured him that she would absorb all the risk. Any curse would fall upon her, not him.

How wrong she was. When Esau realized what Jacob had done, he was angry enough to kill his conniving brother. Rebekah was convinced he would do it too, so she scrambled and sent her favorite son to her brother's house, hundreds of miles away. Rebekah never saw Jacob again. Her family was permanently divided.

A Control Girl rarely counts the cost. She doesn't anticipate the way her children will hate each other. She doesn't picture them moving away and never bringing the grandkids to visit. She never envisions the solitude, heartache, or severed marriage. In her drive to have control, she fails to consider the collateral damage and the potential for a Not-So-Happy Ending.

How to repent: Consider where the Control Girl road is leading. If you spend the next ten years doing what you're doing, what will happen to your relationships? How will each person be affected? Will your family be filled with love and peace or fighting and hatred?

For the sake of the people you love, turn back now. Stop taking control. Protect your friends and family from the painful fallout that is sure to mark their futures. Philippians 2:3–4 says it best: "Do nothing from selfish ambition or conceit, but in humility count others more significant than yourselves. Let each of you look not only to his own interests, but also to the interests of others."

Ladies, God designed us to be cultivators of strong, loving relationships. But by taking control we sabotage, rather than fortify, them. Let's repent of control and turn back before it's too late.

- ❀ Read back through the four ways to repent of control. Ask God to convict your heart and bring to mind anything you have been blind to.

- ❀ Make a plan of action. Write it down. List out the ways God is prompting you to build peace between the people you love.

For Meditation: Proverbs 6:12–19

By eavesdropping, pitting people against each other, being deceitful, or ignoring the risk of collateral damage, I create a miserable ending, not the happy one I envision. *Father, I will turn back now, and stop using controlling tactics.*

Lesson 5: Standing for God Versus Standing In for Him
Read Genesis 27:1–45

MY HUSBAND AND I disagree about his glasses. I think he should wear them. He thinks wearing them will cause his eyesight to deteriorate, so he only wears them to drive. The eye doctor is a nice guy, but he sides with my husband and says the glasses are only essential for driving—which I have trouble believing. If the glasses can bring new crispness to road signs and lines on the highway, wouldn't they also be helpful for bringing sharper focus to the rest of the world?

Though this is a charged topic for us, it's relatively stress-free compared to some of the other things I've gotten all hot and bothered about in the past nineteen years of marriage. It's not good for my blood pressure to recount them all, but you know the sort of "discussions" I'm talking about.

Maybe you have a few points of contention in your own marriage. Perhaps your husband is opposed to having another baby, and you desperately crave one. Or you'd like him to go to church with you. Or give your daughter a hug once in a while. Or stop watching so much football.

If you're like me, the more convinced you are that God is on your side of the argument, the greater the temptation to take control. I can't make a strong case that God wants Ken to wear his glasses. But when I'm convinced God *is* on my side of an issue, I feel quite comfortable standing in for him and speaking to my husband on God's behalf. I think of myself as God's Control Girl, at his service.

This sort of attitude, I believe, is what ensnared Rebekah. Her husband was not only physically blind, but she was convinced he was spiritually blind as well. Rebekah was absolutely positive that God wanted their younger son, Jacob, to receive the blessing. God told her so. He said, "Two nations are in your womb, and . . . the older shall serve the younger" (Gen. 25:23).

Isaac had stubbornly discarded the prophecy, defiantly grooming the customary firstborn, Esau, to be his successor. Now that Isaac's health was deteriorating, the time for the long-disputed blessing had come. But rather than scheduling a face-off with Rebekah, Isaac did what men often do. He avoided her.

THE BLESSING

In those days, the birthright—which involved dividing property—was firmly rooted in tradition; everyone knew what to expect. But the blessing was different. It possessed an element of mystery. Entire families would gather to listen in as the patriarch described the future he foresaw for his descendants. Genesis 49 records the blessing that, decades later, Jacob speaks over his sons, predicting the future of each one.

But in lieu of a ceremonious family gathering, the twins' father, Isaac, schedules a *private* blessing with Esau. Only Esau. His plan is to indulge in the food he loves before he blesses the son he loves, and he doesn't want Rebekah interfering.

From backstage, we listen in as Isaac blesses the son he presumes is Esau. He says, "Be lord over your brothers, and may your mother's sons bow down to you" (Gen. 27:29). Our jaws drop incredulously as we recognize these words. This is the prophecy that God spoke over Jacob before he was born. And now, Isaac has spoken the same prophecy—unknowingly—over Jacob as well.

Did Isaac really think he could slip this blessing past God? He reminds me of a toddler who thinks no one can see him if he is in the corner with his eyes closed.

How Rebekah must have chortled gleefully as she heard the blessing fall from her husband's lips onto the *rightful* son. She had prevailed over this critical moment in her family's history. She had taken control. But as Rebekah fist pumps backstage, what is God's response? Does he lean down from heaven to give her a high five?

Hardly. This dark moment stems directly from Eve's curse. Rebekah's heart is bent on taking control, and her perspective on what is good and right is severely distorted. In one sense, she is taking a stand for God, but her methods are deplorable. This was the work of a woman who doubted that God was in control. It's the work of a Control Girl.

A Trembling Man

With the door still swinging behind trickster Jacob, in comes Esau with another meal, hot and ready, but Isaac is surprised. If this is Esau, whom did he just bless?

Then it hits him. His plan is foiled. He hasn't succeeded in overriding God's prophecy. His older son will serve his younger. In spite of Isaac's discreet, secret plotting, God has prevailed. And how does Isaac respond? He trembles. Violently.

Proverbs says that "the fear of the LORD is the beginning of wisdom" (9:10), and Isaac's trembling marks a turning point. As it's all dawning on him, Isaac's statement, "Yes, and he shall be blessed," is like a midsentence U-turn (Gen. 27:33). He not only recognizes that God *is* going to bless Jacob, but he accepts it with fear and trembling and aligns himself with God.[2]

It's important to note that Isaac was trembling before God, not Rebekah. His surrender to God happened in spite of what his controlling, conniving wife had done, not because of it.[3]

Playing God

No wife can railroad her husband into surrendering to God, though Rebekah sure did try. When a Control Girl, convinced that she represents God's agenda, begins hounding her husband, she'll only cause him to resist in sullen anger. This pattern is also true in other relationships. A woman who tries to stand in for God as a friend, parent, employee, or boss often creates tension and resistance.

God doesn't ask me to browbeat others into obeying him, especially not my husband, whom God has told me to respect. First Peter 3:1–2 says, "Even if [husbands] do not obey the word, they may be won without a word . . . when they see your respectful and pure conduct." According to this verse, a wife *should* try to win her husband to God's ways. But she must do so winsomely, respectfully, and with pure motives. This, her husband will respond to. If she tries to control him and corral him for God, he'll just stubbornly resist.

In his book *Love and Respect*, Emerson Eggerichs notices that women often see themselves as spiritually superior to their husbands. Wives often try to "play God," but Eggerichs rarely hears a husband say, "I've got to stop being my wife's personal Holy Spirit." Men tend to stonewall under their wives' spiritual scrutiny, not the other way around.[4]

This was true for Rebekah's marriage . . . and mine.

CHERYL'S ADVICE

Years ago, I secretly felt spiritually superior to my husband. During worship, he showed no emotion. Instead of joining a study group, he plodded along with daily Bible reading. His prayers seemed monotonous compared to my dynamic, expressive ones. I thought he was spiritually dry. So whenever we disagreed about what God wanted for our family, I struggled to let him lead. Wasn't I more qualified?

I decided to broach the subject with a godly mentor. I said, "Cheryl, you seem so spiritually strong. Has there ever been a time that you struggled with your husband lagging a bit?"

She told me that her husband's spiritual maturity was not inferior to but different from hers. She said he liked studying the Bible's facts and details, and his dedication to God was methodical. Then she told me about a time that she was so sick she almost died. She talked about how fiercely loyal her husband had been, and how he fought for the medical attention that ultimately saved her life.

Cheryl said her husband *became* her spiritual life. She was too weak to pray, read her Bible, or even think clearly. He supplied the only thoughts that she could hang on to. She clearly remembers him reminding her that no one could snatch her out of God's hand (John 10:29). She concluded by saying, "I appreciate him just the way he is." Her wisdom was profound.

I haven't had a brush with death like Cheryl, but I've noticed that in times of weakness, I most appreciate my husband's faith. I see a correlation between my attitude and his spiritual responsiveness. When I scrutinize my husband's relationship with God, he stonewalls, which only causes me to judge him more. But when I humble *myself* and invite his spiritual input, he becomes the man of faith I'm craving.

Ken still doesn't raise his hands when he sings or cry when he prays. But God never asked me to stand over my husband with *my* version of a spiritual checklist. God has a relationship with Ken; he doesn't need me to stand in for him.

I wonder how Rebekah's story might have ended if she hadn't stood in for God. What if she had quietly surrendered to God? What if she had fiercely trusted him with the future, rather than pouncing on her husband's manipulative plans?

We can't write an alternate ending for Rebekah's story, but we can for ourselves. God will have his way with our families, just as he did with Rebekah's. He doesn't need our Control Girl help. He's got this.

❁   What are the three biggest ongoing points of contention in your marriage (or other relationship)? Do you consider God to be on your side of the argument?

❁   When have you "stood in" for God? How did others react?

For Meditation: 1 Peter 3:1–2

I cannot railroad anyone into surrendering to God. *Lord, I commit to stop trying to stand in for you.*

Rebekah's Unhappy Ending

REBEKAH'S LOVE STORY unfurled like a rose, but its beauty wilted over time.

When it seemed that Rebekah's husband would undo the prophecy spoken over their twin boys, she feared the worst. Rather than trusting God's sovereignty, which had shaped her life so far, Rebekah took control using deception and disguise. She tricked her husband and sealed the fate of her favorite son—the one God had chosen. But in doing so, she also sealed her own misery.

Her beloved son fled from his raging brother, and she never saw him again. For the rest of her life Rebekah lived inside the Unhappy Ending she created. If only she had waited on the Lord rather than standing in for him. If only we would do the same.

Chapter Six
Leah: Invisible and Unloved

LEAH'S STORY has a dark, foreboding beginning. She had an evil father and was forced to live in the dreary shadows of her beautiful little sister. To the men in Leah's life, she was invisible, unloved, and worthless. She was a girl stuck in a story that was out of her control, and there was nothing she could do about it.

Through her tears, Leah couldn't see that there was Someone else looking on, lovingly, from a distance. He saw great value in her, and his eyes glimmered with anticipation of the grandeur to come . . .

Lesson 1: An Invisible Bride
Read Genesis 29:1–31

SOMETIMES, WHEN WE look back at things that were out of our control—such as being mistreated or overlooked as a child—we are tempted to doubt whether God truly was or is in control. Did he see what happened there in the darkness? Does he care?

Natalie had an extremely painful childhood. As a little girl she would go absolutely berserk, breaking glass and hitting herself with objects, trying to make her dad "see" her. But he just looked straight through her, sometimes for days. It was his way of punishing her for displeasing him. Natalie learned that she could sometimes get him to notice her, though, if she rubbed against his pants.

Since Natalie was trained by her father to doubt her own worth, when she started dating she gravitated to boys who devalued her. One such boyfriend caused Natalie such severe despair that she attempted suicide.

After she woke up in the hospital, her first concern was whether her dad knew. And though he did show up at the hospital, he didn't make eye contact with or speak to Natalie. Afterward, he never mentioned the suicide attempt. In many ways, Natalie still feels invisible to her dad.

A dad plays no small role in the development of a girl's self-worth. When a dad is cold, demanding, abusive, or absent, his little girl tends to question her value and think, *I must be worthless. Why else would my own dad treat me this way?*[1]

BRIDE-PRICE

Leah's dad was a cold, narcissistic man who used people. For Laban, a daughter's worth was based on what bride-price she would bring. And Rachel, Leah's beautiful sister, was sure to bring far more than Leah.

One day, Rachel came bursting through the door with news that her cousin, Jacob, was at the well. Laban probably salivated on the spot, remembering years ago, when a servant from the same family had come with gold bracelets for his sister. Had Jacob come with similar bridal gifts?

Turns out, Jacob was traveling light, sporting only his rippling muscles to impress young Rachel with. But impressed she was. A month later they were engaged. In exchange for Rachel's hand, Laban accepted Jacob's offer of seven years' labor, a two-carat diamond in that day's economy of marriage proposals. But Jacob was happy to pay the exorbitant bride-price. His passion for Rachel made the years pass like days (Gen. 29:20).[2]

For Leah, they must have passed like centuries. Seven years is a long time for jealousy to fester in the heart of a girl who hovers in the shadows while her sunny sister makes wedding plans. Seven years of would-be suitors looking past her. Seven years of two-carat Rachel bringing a gleam to Daddy's greedy eyes. Seven years of zero-carat Leah feeling invisible and worthless in everyone's eyes.

Swallowed in Darkness

Laban used those seven years to formulate his next conniving move. On the day of the wedding, with guests gathered and wine flowing, he did the unthinkable. He swapped out the bride without telling the groom.

We can assume it was dark, Jacob was drunk, and Leah was heavily veiled as Laban escorted her (not Rachel) to the bridal chamber. Any *good* father would rescue a daughter from such a situation. But Laban escorted Leah into it.

Laban was all about revenue. His plan let him to offload Leah and double his profit on her pretty sister. It was a win-win. But for Leah, it was a lose-lose. What a message to absorb. *So my dad thinks the only way he'll ever get rid of me is by tricking someone into marrying me. I'm the girl nobody wants. Nobody loves. Not even my own father.* It was a whole new level of shame.

How it must have pierced Leah's heart to hear Jacob's voice, thick with desire, whispering her sister's name and not her own in the darkness. But what could she do? Reveal her identity and betray her father? Suppose she *did* interrupt the groom, hungrily groping her body, and say, "Uh . . . excuse me. It's Leah, here." What then? Would he recoil in disgust? Certainly he would march Leah right back to her father and demand his *real* bride. And that was sure to spark the least happy ending of all: a hopeless future tethered to an irate father.

So Leah stayed quiet. She didn't let on. She let Jacob believe that she was someone else. She let herself become even more invisible, swallowed in the darkness of Jacob's bed.

Pain as deep as Leah's can absolutely define you. It can set a course for the future. You vow to never let someone hurt you like that again. You put up walls, withdraw, numb yourself to relationships, or limit yourself to superficiality. You become rigidly independent to prove you don't need people. Or you become a producer. A perfectionist. You throw yourself into your work, ministry, or appearance to define your worth. You attract new girlfriends who think you're fun, new men who think you're sexy.

None of these attempts to ward off feelings of worthlessness are overtly controlling. But there is a defensive aspect to control, isn't there? We might project confidence, rigidity, or independence, when inside we're just hurting. We're trying to defend ourselves against being hurt again. And while it's not bad to keep others from controlling us, sometimes defensiveness becomes a destructive pattern. We guard against everyone. We trust no one. Including God.

Eventually, we'll watch Leah try to take control of her out-of-control situation. She tries desperately to regain her sense of worth, which was so invalidated by her father. Behind her actions, we can almost hear Leah screaming, "Somebody see me! Love me! Value me!" She didn't realize that Somebody already did.

He Saw Me

There is a line in Leah's story that punches a hole in the darkness of despair. It says, "The Eternal One saw how Leah was unloved" (Gen. 29:31 VOICE). He *saw* her. He cared enough to keep an eye on her, and he was close enough to detect her mistreatment.

No matter how invisible you feel, you are not invisible to God. Even in your darkest moments of deepest shame, when another person has used or discarded you, when the whole world glares at you or passes by as if you're invisible, God sees you. As surely as he saw Leah, he sees you.

But will this make any difference to you? It's your choice. You can go on withering under the glaring scorn of others. You can be controlled by what they do or don't think. Or you can step out of the shadows and bask in the realization that there is another set of eyes on you: God's. He sees you, accepts you, and invites you to draw near. He truly loves you.

Remember Natalie, who felt invisible as a child? Recently, Natalie's mind began unlocking childhood memories. It was so painful that Natalie turned to God in a way she never had before. Suddenly, it dawned on Natalie that these new details from her past weren't new to God. He had been right there all along. *He* had seen her, even when her father hadn't. He had loved her, even when her dad clearly didn't.

Natalie realized that her dad might never look at her with the affection and acceptance she's been craving for so long. But to know that a Father's eyes, filled with love, have been resting on her all along is like soothing ointment on open wounds.

Friends, God sees you too. Today, a line of sight can be drawn between God's eyes and you. He values you and loves you. Let that thought punch a hole in your darkness and spread like ointment on your wounded heart. Don't spend your life trying to get people to see you correctly. Let *God* be the Daddy who sees and determines your worth. Trust what he says about you rather than what hurtful people say. This is one significant way of giving him control.

- ❀ Think back to the darkest moments of your life. Now, picture God looking on with eyes filled with love. How does this make you feel?

- ❀ List the ways you try to make people see you correctly. Above your list, write the words, "God sees me. He loves me."

- ❀ Read Isaiah 43:1–4 and write down any messages the Lord has for you about your worth.

For Meditation: Isaiah 43:4

Other people might look right through me, but I will let God be the Daddy who determines my worth. *God, I believe that you see me, value me, and love me.*

Lesson 2: An Unveiled Bride
Read Genesis 29:16–30

WHEN MY DAUGHTER was two, she grabbed a tube of my lipstick, headed for the bathroom mirror, and said, "I gonna go get all pretty." But when she looked into the mirror, before she ever touched the makeup to her lips, she said, "Oh. I is all pretty!" What a sweet contrast to the way most women look into the mirror. We're usually discouraged or frustrated by what we see, not pleasantly surprised.

I imagine Leah didn't enjoy mirrors. She wasn't beautiful. The Bible mentions her eyes. Perhaps they were crossed or protruding.[3] Whatever the cause, Scripture holds her in stark contrast to her younger sister who *was* beautiful.

Did you know that Leah's name means "cow," and Rachel's name means "lamb"?[4] It's hard enough to be the "cow," but when your baby sister is the darling, little lamb, it's exponentially more difficult. Especially when your new husband, on his wedding night, thinks he's climbed into bed with the little lamb, and "in the morning, behold, it was Leah!" (Gen. 29:25).

Imagine that moment for Leah. Had she lain awake all night in dread, loathing what was sure to come next? Then it happened. Her new husband stirred. He turned to her. And the morning sunlight ripped open the reality of the night before.

That image of Jacob's horror-stricken face at the sight of her must have burned itself permanently into Leah's memory. Did he jump up in panicky disgust, getting tangled in the sheets? Did he run out, half dressed?

Jacob found Leah's dad and demanded to know why he had been deceived. Laban's response was thick with implication: "Around here, we don't put the younger first."[5] He was drawing attention to the way Jacob slipped away with Esau's firstborn privileges. But noble Laban wasn't going to let that happen here. No, sir. If Jacob wanted pretty Rachel, he'd have to start by marrying ugly, firstborn Leah.

How humiliating for Leah. Her new groom recoils at the sight of her.

Her father gloats at having tricked Jacob into marrying her. And now her shame of being unwanted is on display for the wedding guests. All because she lacked the beauty that Rachel had.

THE BOSSY MIRROR

Good thing *we* don't live in such a harsh world, where our worth is calculated by our appearance, right? (Insert sarcastic laughter.) From behind a billion screens, all flickering gorgeous displays of photo-enhanced women, our culture screams, "Do you want to be worth something? Do you want to have a happy life filled with admiring people and endless opportunities? Then be beautiful. Beauty is your way to take control of your destiny."

So we go after beauty with a vengeance. Maybe there was nothing Leah could do, but *we* have lots of options. We run in circles between the gym, the mall, and the salon. But even after we've beaten ourselves into submission on the treadmill and spent every last cent on cosmetic surgery, that bossy, reflective glass on the wall still finds flaws. It points sharply to new fat dimples, sagging skin, and wrinkles. If anything, our beauty seems to be fading. We're losing control, not gaining it.

The more we strain to achieve physical perfection, the more we fall prey to perfectionism, eating disorders, anxiety, and depression. It's the irony all Control Girls face. **The thing we use to gain control ultimately ends up controlling us**.

In our self-consciousness, we resort to using veils. We dye our gray hair, spread on makeup, wear shape-inducing underwear, and buy age-defying serums. These aren't necessarily wrong, of course. Unless our goal is to take control by dressing up and tricking someone into valuing us like Laban did with Leah.

REJECTED BY HIM

Of all the eyes that scrutinize us, there's often one pair that we agonize over most. Those eyes belonging to the man you've given yourself to. What if *he* rejects you?

Maybe he already has. Perhaps your husband walked in while you were changing and made a face of disgust. Maybe he stopped putting his arm around you or even looking at you, after your face was scarred in the accident. Maybe your fiancé broke up with you, just after the chemo stripped you of your hair. Or your baby's father abandoned you when your shape changed.

Rejection like that is bitter, painful, and sickening. It's a loss of control that leaves us devastatingly vulnerable. For Leah, the stinging slap of rejection from her husband wasn't a passing moment. There was more to come, starting with the honeymoon. Leah's dad said Jacob could have Rachel, but only after he finished out the week sleeping with Leah. How romantic.

How Leah must have suffered, knowing her groom was there out of obligation rather than delight. Was he thinking of her sister while they were in bed together? A woman married to a porn addict knows what this rejection is like. Her husband may be with her physically, but his mind is captured by the plastic look of desire on another woman's face. He is ensnared by airbrushed perfection, and there's nothing the *real* woman in his bed can do to win him back.

Oh, my poor tormented sisters, let me coax you out of the shadows of shame, rejection, and insecurity. Step away from the mirror, the scale, the man, anything that stirs up feelings of humiliation in your soul. Let's look at your reflection in a new mirror, shall we?

UNVEILED

If you are a Christian, you are the bride of Christ, and your Bridegroom—Jesus—is nothing like Jacob. Leah had plenty to stress about in anticipation of her groom's first glimpse under the veil. But when Jesus pulls your bridal veil back, you have no reason to shrink back or hide from his gaze. You are loved and wanted! Your Bridegroom paid an extravagant amount to have you as his own. He laid down his life so that you could be his!

And here's the most amazing part: Jesus chose you and he chose me while our ugliness was in full view. Not outside ugliness—that's not what Jesus looks at. His eyes penetrate beneath the layers we add, and he sees the hidden person of our heart (1 Peter 3:4). So even when my inner person was covered in hairy warts, Jesus chose me. Not because I *was* beautiful, but because he wanted to *make* me beautiful.

Jesus is the opposite of selfish Jacob, who focused on externals. Jesus was selfless. He gave his life to wash our hearts, make us clean, and draw us close (Rom. 5:8; Eph. 5:25–26). Remember how the thick, heavy veil in the temple tore from top to bottom just after Jesus died? This served as an invitation for us to come boldly into God's presence as the newly purchased brides of God's Son. We don't have to wither in shame the way Leah did. We are officially accepted (Mark 15:38; Heb. 10:19–23).

Drawing close to God is what transforms us into a beautiful bride for Christ. It's like when Moses's face glowed after spending time with God on the mountain. The Bible is compared to a mirror that shows us the hidden person of our hearts, the part we primp for Jesus. When we spend time in this "mirror," we come away reflecting Christ's beauty (Exod. 34:29–35; 2 Cor. 3:17–18; James 1:23–25).

A NEW MIRROR

Friends, let me ask a question that might sting a bit: Who are you dressing for?

Jesus, your Bridegroom, looks at you differently than any man ever has. So what does it say to him when you spend time dejectedly glaring into that sharp, critical piece of glass on the bathroom wall? What message does it send when you're obsessed with losing weight or urgent about dyeing your hair? If Jesus knows the number of hairs on your head, he certainly knows what color they are beneath the highlights.

Picture a woman stepping onto the scale. The number is up. She turns to the mirror and notices that her skin seems to sag more than yesterday. There are new wrinkles near her eyes, and her muffin top shows beneath her blouse. But she doesn't turn frantically to apply more makeup or change her clothes. Instead, she turns to the mirror of God's Word.

She settles there, in God's presence, assuring herself of Christ's love.

Rapidly, her insecurities begin to melt away. She's filled with peace, joy, and love, which show up on her face. See how Christ's image begins to mingle with hers in the mirror? See how he's honored by her healthy glow?

Others might not remark about her beautiful figure or skin. They might never call her "striking." But they do see something lovely in her gracious, caring ways. With every year that passes, her glow brightens as she reflects the love of her Bridegroom.

Control Girl, you might be stuck in what feels like Leah's honeymoon. The rejection and humiliation never stop, and you have no control. Is there anything you can do? Yes. Step away from the mirror the world waves in your face. Look instead into the mirror that makes you glow. Put God, and no one else, in control of deciding your worth.

* How does your fear or agitation in the mirror indicate a deeper struggle for control?

* Are you plagued by perfectionism, anxiety, depression, or eating disorders? Are you obsessed with fashion, fitness, or anti-aging techniques? How has your desire for control begun to control you?

* Read Hebrews 10:19–23, listing any descriptive words or phrases in the verses. Which ones describe you? How so?

For Meditation: Hebrews 10:22

I don't have to live under the rejection and humiliation of the world's mirror. When I settle myself in front of the mirror of God's Word, my insecurities melt away, and I become beautiful. *God, I give you control by letting you decide my worth.*

Lesson 3: Before I Can Give God Control
Read Genesis 29:31–35

LEAH SMOOTHS HER hair with a trembling hand. Forcing herself to smile into the mirror, she takes a breath and whispers, "Jacob is going to be so pleased. This baby is *perfect*." She leans down and kisses the tiny nose of her sleeping infant. "Your daddy is going to love you," she says softly, choking back tears. "And he's going to love me too."

Leah named her first baby Reuben, which means, "See, a son." It's as if she's holding out her brand-new baby to Jacob, saying, "See! Jacob, do you see? A son!" Desperate for Jacob's approval, Leah says, "Now my husband will love me" (Gen. 29:32).

Somehow, I don't think the scene played out the way Leah had hoped, for she names her second son Simeon, which sounds like "heard" in Hebrew. She explains, "Because the LORD has heard that I am hated" (Gen. 29:33).

Then Leah named her third son Levi, which sounds like "attached" in Hebrew. She explains, "Now this time my husband will be attached to me, because I have borne him three sons" (Gen. 29:34).

Look at the way Leah enslaves herself to Jacob. She recognizes that God is compassionately blessing her with these babies, but her eyes are not on God. She is fixated on Jacob. She lays baby after baby before him, hoping to see some glimmer of acceptance or endearment. She gives Jacob—not God—the role of deciding her worth.

I believe Leah could have birthed twenty sons, and Jacob still would have remained as detached and uncaring as he was on that fateful morning in their marriage bed. Leah reminds me of a little child who keeps bringing her lunch money to the bully, longing to be accepted. Or a battered wife who keeps setting hot meals and baskets of clean laundry before her abusive husband, desperate for his affection. Or a depressed teen who keeps giving up little pieces of her individuality, craving approval from her peers.

We want to shake the victimized person and say, "Why do you let them control you like this?" But we could look in the mirror and ask the same question.

Like Leah, we hold up our children, our work, our accomplishments, saying, "Hey, world! Do you see what I've produced? Do I matter to you now?" We might garner a bit of praise or admiration, but this quickly expires. The watching world forgets us and becomes enamored with some other, more impressive person. Astonishingly, the dejection only fuels our next attempt to gain approval.

By staking our worth in what others think, without realizing it, we've let them control us.

THE IRONY OF CONTROL

God says he should be in control of our lives and that it should matter most what he thinks. But somehow, it seems more freeing to yank the controller from God's hands and put it in the hands of someone we can see: a husband, sibling, boss, or peer group.

Again, our problem with control is ironic. The more desperate we are to be accepted, the more control we give to others. We don't mean to give them control, but unwittingly we do when we allow their opinions to matter so much. We give them what they want, so that they will give us what we want: the relief of finally being accepted. Like Leah, we repeatedly bring our gifts and sacrifices to our new master, saying, "Maybe this time he'll notice. Maybe this time he'll appreciate me."

But our gifts are never enough. Our master is never pleased. We wither under his glaring scorn, or self-loath after we don't measure up. Our so-called path to freedom is lined with self-defeating patterns and destructive relationships, all because we let someone else's opinion matter more than God's. Why do we allow ourselves to be controlled in this way? And how can we ever break free?

A CONTROLLING MOTHER

For Audra, giving God his rightful place involved refusing to be controlled by her mother. Audra has tried desperately to please her mom. Whenever her mom became *dis*pleased about something, Audra felt compelled to find a solution. She felt indebted, somehow, to her mom.

Audra's desire to please her mom became like an addiction, w negatively affected her other relationships. Her mom always came t Audra even bought her mom a house and paid its mortgage for decade Then, when Audra faced financial challenges and needed to sell t house to keep herself afloat, her mother became irate. She was ang and resentful toward Audra, and told friends that Audra was throw her out of her own house.

The worst part came after the house sold. Though Audra paid for mo ers and tried to help with packing, her mom was spiteful and belligerent She wouldn't talk to Audra and left behind heaps of unwanted belongings. Those weeks of working to get the house ready for closing were some of the most physically and emotionally grueling days of Audra's life.

Audra now sees that her indebtedness toward her mom was unhealthy. She had lived in bondage, trying to win her mom's approval. But no matter how much she gave, Audra could never make her mom completely happy. Only God can do that.

For Audra, giving control to God has included refusing to be controlled by her mom. It's been painful to break free from old patterns, but Audra is finding new freedom in her relationship with God. Now when she prays for her mom, she says, "If it be your will," and then she leaves her mom's happiness in God's hands rather than taking it upon herself.

We give control to the person whose opinion matters most to us. For each of us, this person needs to be God.

BREAKING FREE

When Leah announces the birth of her fourth son, we see a change in her. She names her baby Judah, which means "praise," saying, "This time I will praise the LORD" (Gen. 29:35). Do you hear the joyful deliverance of her heart? This time, Leah isn't urgently searching Jacob's face for acceptance. This time, her gaze is locked on God. As Leah holds her baby up to the One who blessed her with the gift of motherhood, this time she is free.

All other masters but the one true God will lead us into destructive bondage. They will demand more than we can give and cause our lives to be disordered, broken, and painful. God is the complete opposite. He doesn't insist that we satisfy him by meeting endless demands. He has already *been* satisfied, through his Son who died in our place.

God only asks that we put him first and worship him alone. This might require more than just singing a worship song or saying a peaceful prayer. Putting God first is often a gritty struggle of breaking ourselves free from old masters and old strongholds. But once we do, we're free. Our new Master is nothing like the old tyrannical ones. Jesus offers to take control because he knows that his rule causes our lives to become ordered, satisfying, and joy-filled, just the way he intended them to be.

Friend, have you put your "controller" in another master's hands? If so, you'll need to retrieve it before you can give control to God. Audra had to take control back from her mother. For Leah, it was her husband. Whom do you need to break free from?

❀ List the people you are currently allowing to define your worth. What negative patterns has this produced in you?

❀ Who are you controlled by? How does this keep you from fully surrendering to God?

❀ What steps do you need to take to break free from the control of others? Name one friend who can help support you in this process. Make a plan to reach out for help.

For Meditation: Revelation 5:12

I am not free to fully surrender to God until I stop letting the opinions of others control me. *Lord, I surrender to you by making your opinion (not _____'s) matter most.*

Leah's Happy Ending

LEAH'S STORY, WHICH began in the dreary shadows of her beautiful sister and evil father, did not bode well. Yet God looked on with a glimmer in his eye, knowing that good was in store.

Leah only got to see the beginning of God's rich, satisfying ending for her life. She didn't realize the significant role her fourth son—the one she praised God for—would have in God's overarching story line. Leah's son, Judah, fathered the tribe of Judah, which Jesus was born into. Imagine the grandeur. Leah was the great-great-grandmother of the "Lion of Judah"!

Revelation 5:5 says, "Weep no more; behold, the Lion of the tribe of Judah . . . has conquered." What a message of hope for Leah in that Lion's conquering roar. Yes, her dark beginning was worthy of many tears. She was vulnerable, unloved, and weak. But this verse of prophecy calls to Leah, saying, "Stop weeping and look. The Lion has conquered!" Leah's miserable past is swallowed up in victory. And if you belong to this conquering Lion, yours will be too.

Chapter Seven
Rachel: When She Has More

To Jacob, Rachel was the fairest of them all. The apple of his eye. The prize to be had. She was the kind of girl who made a year's work seem like a day. Rachel's father had been the first to appreciate her spell-casting beauty. He used it like a carrot on the end of Jacob's plow. For fourteen years.

While this might have all been charming at first, it didn't lead to a charmed life. Rachel emerged from childhood with a skewed sense of place. She was entitled, demanding, and controlling. And when it became obvious that she wasn't truly in control, she got uglier still.

Rachel's unsatisfying story is proof that you can be pretty, have the romantic love of an adoring man, and still be miserable.

Lesson 1: Family Demands
Read Genesis 29:16–20, 30–31; 30:1–2, 14–15; 31:33–35

RACHEL IS THE Control Girl who surprised me most. I opened her story with such fondness and anticipation. She was the beautiful woman Jacob adored; I thought of her as "the fairest of them all." But when I actually bit into her story, I found traces of the curse's poison in every scene.

Because Rachel was beautiful, she got what she wanted. Things seemed to go her way. But this was just an illusion of control, and God, who is faithful to invite each Control Girl to himself, created a cord-dangling moment just for Rachel.

Rachel's first recorded words are, "Give me children, or I shall die!" (Gen. 30:1). She's talking to Jacob, and I can't help but picture her hands around his neck as she says it. She is an angry Control Girl, frustrated that she can't get control of her body and make it conceive a baby.

But Rachel wasn't just longing for a baby. Her problem was bigger than that: She wanted to make Jacob a father, to fill her nest with people whose lives were unequivocally attached to hers. She wanted all of the honor and satisfaction associated with having a family.

We can relate to that. Though our culture doesn't emphasize bearing children like Rachel's did, women today still long for a family. We have certain hopes and expectations for how our families should turn out, and if our idea of a Happy Ending is threatened, we often—like Rachel—get our hands around the necks of our loved ones and say, "Give me what I want, or I will die!"

See how those words are laced with manipulation? You wouldn't turn to a total stranger with that threat. You turn to someone who loves you. Someone who wants to please you. Someone you can control. You turn to a family member.

TIES THAT BIND

As we've already discussed, women are particularly gifted in the art of relationships. We use the ties that bind to draw loved ones together.

But because of our cursed desire for control, we also use our relational ties as ropes or even whips. We've cooked their potatoes and washed their socks, and now it's our turn to demand something in return.

There's a common theme in the stories I hear whenever I ask people about the most controlling woman they know. Let's see if you can find it:

- Grace says they can't afford the cruise. But her mother-in-saw says, "We'll pay for it. What's the problem?"
- Lily's mom demands that Christmas be celebrated on December 25 with all children and grandchildren present. No exceptions.
- Monika and her husband are going to Europe for three weeks. Monika's mother expects the kids to spend one day with the other grandma and the rest with her. She explodes when Monika calls this unreasonable.
- Janie receives a text from her mother-in-law. It's the holiday plans with a daily itinerary. Janie knows that none of the events are optional.

Did you catch the theme? It seems like every controlling matriarch of the family is trying to gather everyone together. When one family event concludes, she begins planning the next, each with swelling expectations and demands. If her family resists, she huffs and fumes, saying, "I was just trying to do something *nice* for everyone."

And perhaps that's true, to some extent. But I think there might be another reason. When the stretches between visits get longer and the phone calls get shorter, a fear creeps in. Fear of being forgotten, being lonely, or not mattering to anyone. Fear of being irrelevant.

The Happy Ending we've been craving, from before our children were born, is quite the opposite of this. God wired us to long for meaningful, lasting family relationships. It's why we care so deeply and tug so insistently on the people we love. But when our tug becomes a yank, and our request becomes a demand, rather than drawing everyone in, we drive them away.

When Rachel had Jacob by the neck, she was wrong. And when I have my loved ones by the neck, I'm wrong too. **Rather than demanding that "my people" rescue me from my deepest fears, God wants to be the one I turn to.**

BREAKING THE SECOND COMMANDMENT

I've always had trouble telling the difference between the first two of the Ten Commandments, but Rachel's and Leah's stories bring clarity. The first commandment says, "You shall have no other gods before me" (Exod. 20:3). That's the one Leah broke when she served Jacob and tried to please him, not God.

But Rachel didn't serve Jacob and try desperately to please him. Instead, she demanded that *he* please *her.* The second commandment says, "You shall not make for yourself an idol" (Exod. 20:4 NASB). Author Paula Hendricks defines an idol as anything that, if you don't or can't have it, "you think you'll face a 'hell'—your personal version of torment and pain."[1]

For Rachel, "hell on earth" was infertility. She loathed the idea of living her whole life without the dignity, security, and respect that children would bring. And who could save her from this hell? Her husband. So she turned to him, and said, "Give me a baby, or I'll die!"

But Jacob responded, saying, "Am I God?" And he was right. Babies come from God, not husbands. Only God can save us from our worst fears.

A FRANTIC CONTROL GIRL

The Bible records several instances of Rachel scratching and clawing after a baby. In her desperation to escape her dread of childlessness, she turns everywhere but to God.

In Genesis 30:14–15, we're privy to a conversation between Rachel and her sister, revealing that Rachel was monopolizing Jacob's bed and not sharing him with the other three wives. Now, to be clear, God doesn't support polygamy. But neither did he endorse Rachel when she handed out "Sleep with Jacob" schedules with her name beside every date. It's another example of Control Girl Rachel demanding that Jacob "save" her.

Out of desperation, Rachel agreed to trade a night with Jacob for Leah's mandrakes (plant roots thought to improve fertility). So Rachel momentarily loosened her grip on her Jacob-idol, but only because she was reaching for a plant-idol.

Genesis 31:33–35 tells of another blatant instance of Rachel's idolatry. This time, she stole her father's gods, which she probably thought offered protection and fertility. But when her dad came after the gods, Rachel sat on them and made an excuse about having her period to keep them hidden. So Rachel was *sitting* on her new object of hope. What a pathetic substitute for God.

Rachel's desire for family was by God's design. God is the one who causes us to love babies and long for motherhood. And every baby born is knit together in a mother's womb by God. Yet, in spite of this, Rachel went everywhere *but* to God with her deepest fears and cravings. The Bible mentions no instance of Rachel ever turning to him.

It's hard to call Rachel's acts of desperation idolatry, but when we turn to anything but God to be "saved," we turn to an idol. God hates idolatry, partly because of what it does to *us*. Putting our hope in someone or something other than God causes us to become more controlling. We clamp tighter and become more demanding. We clench the throats of those we hope will "save" us. And we make everybody miserable with our fanaticism.

Friends, what if we relinquished control? What if, rather than using the ties that bind to push, demand, and control, we let God be in control? What if we let him write the Happy Ending—starting with us?

FEAST NIGHT

My mom has worked very hard over many years to relinquish control. Our family is just as important to her as any other mom or grandma on the block, but rather than making us an idol, Mom repeatedly turns to God and gives her fears to him. Rather than demanding or controlling, Mom focuses on serving.

Over the past decade, my husband and kids have spent Monday nights at my parents' house while I teach piano lessons. They call it "feast night" because Mom loads up the table with piles of homemade food like they never see at home. She doesn't do this in a begrudging or resentful way; she is delighted to serve them.

This year, when I decided to take a break from piano lessons, I figured feast night would become a pleasant memory. But my family (including Ken) revolted. The kids said, "Mamaw will still have us. I know she will!" Sheepishly, I asked Mom if she still wanted them to come on Mondays while I attended a Bible study. She said, "I already told them I did!" Isn't that so sweet?

I wonder what would have happened if my mom *demanded* that our family be at her table every Monday night. What if she pressured or guilted everyone into coming? I doubt my kids would be insisting that feast night at their grandparents' house continue.

See how it works? When we demand that our families come and be what we need them to be, they resist. They feel pressured. They sense that we're trying to control them. But when we relinquish control and serve unselfishly with delight, they *want* to come.

That's the kind of grandma I want to be someday. It's the kind of mom and wife I want to be today. I know that I could easily turn my loved ones into idols, grasping their necks and demanding they save me from my worst fears. But God wants to save me both from my fears and from becoming a desperate, controlling woman.

* Would your loved ones describe you as someone who serves cheerfully, or one who applies pressure and tries to control?

* What is your personal version of "hell on earth"? What pain do you dread most, and who or what do you believe will "save" you from this? List out your responses, with God's help.

* Read Psalm 16. Record everything it says about false gods. Record all the Happy Ending promises for those who seek God.

For Meditation: Psalm 16:11

When I clamp onto my family, demanding that they meet my needs, they resist. When I serve unselfishly, they are drawn to me. *God, I trust you with my deepest fears and cravings.*

Lesson 2: Compared to Her

Read Genesis 29:31–30:24

"WHY SO GLUM?" asked my husband. "You're usually so cheerful after Angela visits." It was true. Usually I am. This time, I said, "Yeah . . . I don't think I like Angela anymore."

My husband looked quizzical. "You love Angela," he said. "What happened?" After sorting out my emotions, I realized that my frustration was based on the way, during the entire visit, Angela's kids had been so *good*. They had spent the pretty summer days splashing in the pool, doing little crafts, and chatting cheerfully. Once, two of the girls bumped into each other, then giggled and hugged.

My kids, on the other hand, managed to keep a string of arguments going the whole time. Jockeying for attention, they criticized each other's ideas, interrupted each other's stories, and used lots of shoving for emphasis. In comparison, my parenting came up short, and I didn't like that. Which meant I didn't like *her*. Which now seems utterly ridiculous.

Spending time with Angela makes me a better mom, but only when I refrain from envy. To stop envy, you have to back up and stop what caused it: comparison. Envy always takes the same path. You compare, you feel inadequate, you envy.

It's especially hard when it's obvious that *God* gave the other person something that he didn't give to you. You can't go out and buy it, achieve it, or make it. God gave it to them. You have very little control. See how envy and control are linked? If you were in control, you'd even things out. Your kids would behave nicely like your friend's kids. Your figure would be fabulous like your friend's figure. Your house would be awesome like your friend's house.

Yet so many of these things are beyond our control. Which creates so many opportunities for envy.

TUG-OF-WAR

Rachel's situation was rough. Having babies was incredibly important to women in her day, and Rachel couldn't have any. Yet every time

Rachel lifted her tent flap she saw Leah's latest baby bump getting bigger. It fueled her envy and kicked off a giant tug-of-war match, with each sister heaving, yanking, and straining to fill her side with the most babies: "I [Rachel] have had to wrestle with my own sister as I've wrestled with God, but I have prevailed" (Gen. 30:8 VOICE).

Rachel included God in her wrestling match. He was over on Leah's side. But Rachel dug in her heels, heaved on the rope, and won the match. See? She's got a baby (from her servant Bilhah) in her arms to prove it.

It's so easy to adopt this thinking. Whenever God gives something to my opponent on the other end of the rope, it *feels* like he's against me. And when I strain and yank, and finally get what I want, it feels like I've tugged that rope right out of God's hands.

But God's hands are too big and too wise to be influenced by the tugging of my scrawny Control Girl hands. God gives and takes away, not based on my perspective of good, but his. He is "for" both sides of my tug-of-war rope. In fact, he wants me to put down the rope altogether.

THE COMPARISON "GAME"

It's interesting that people often call comparison a game. It's not. **Comparison is a strategy of war that Satan uses against us.** James 3:14–15 says, "But if you have bitter jealousy and selfish ambition in your hearts . . . this is not the wisdom that comes down from above, but is earthly, unspiritual, demonic."

So comparison is *demonic*? You betcha. Satan's agenda is to polarize and pit us against each other. He gets us to compare, knowing that we'll emerge with either an inferiority or superiority complex. Either way, he puts us in opposite corners, or on opposite sides of the rope.

Satan will always want me to compare myself to Angela, feel inferior, and pull back from the friendship. But Jesus wants the opposite. In Christ, we celebrate the diversity of our spiritual gifts, which are meant to create unity among believers who depend on each other, not superiority or inferiority complexes. It is the enemy, not Jesus, who whispers, "Look at her . . . Compared to her you're a total failure." Or, "Compared to her, you're doing great."

Satan hands out tug-of-war rope like it's a game because he wants to pit us against each other. But God says to drop the rope, stop comparing, and be free.

GOD'S RESPONSE TO RACHEL

After each round of Rachel and Leah's tug-of-war match, the winner gives a brief victory speech as she adds another baby to her side of the rope. Rachel's words describe her vantage point from her tiny window of perspective on life, herself, and God. But let's get on the other side of Rachel's window and look at her situation from God's perspective as well.

> Rachel (after her servant gave birth to Dan): "God has judged me, and has also heard my voice and given me a son." (Gen. 30:6)

> God: "Oh, Rachel . . . infertility isn't my way of giving you a low score. By withholding children, I was tipping your chin up that you might focus on *me*. Yes, I did hear your plea, but I have blessed you with a *baby*, not a tally mark for your side of the contest."

> Rachel (after her servant gave birth to Naphtali): "I have had to wrestle with my own sister as I've wrestled with God, but I have prevailed." (Gen. 30:8 VOICE)

> God: "Rachel, Rachel . . . you are worried and upset about many things. By wrestling against your sister, yes, you do wrestle against me, but not the way that you think. It is your enemy who would have you wrestling, always in a state of agitation. When you get caught up in feeling inferior or superior, it is the enemy who prevails. I'm the one who is *for* you. I want you to stop comparing, let me have control, and find contentment and peace."

Rachel (when she gave birth to Joseph): "God has taken away my reproach." (Gen. 30:23)

God: "Dear Rachel . . . I am not a God who shames his people. Your shame comes from locking your gaze on your sister, comparing yourself with her, grasping for the things I have not given. This baby will bring honor to your name, but not because you have done something great. *I* am doing something great. I will lift Joseph from the lowest pits to the highest places of honor. *That's* the kind of God I am."

TWIN SISTERS

Recently, I watched some little girls playing on a playground. One tiny blond with adorable dimples was gregariously telling a story to her fan club gathered around her. If my friend hadn't pointed her out, I never would have known that another girl, opposite in every way, was the little blond's twin. The taller twin, who was painfully shy, looked on from a distance with obvious irritation. With dark, calculating eyes, she watched a little girl swing around her sister in a playful dance, then whisper in her ear, giggling. You could just see the envy simmering in the sister's soul. Why did everyone look so adoringly at her twin? Why didn't they look at her that way?

I wondered what would happen to this jealous twin. Would she one day blame God, saying, "Why did you give more to her than me?" Would she spend her life tugging vigorously at her end of the "rope" with academics, fitness, or wealth, trying to pull glances of approval and adoration her way?

I wanted to call her over, put my hands on the sides of her face, and say, "Oh, honey . . . stop comparing. Jesus made you special too! He loves you and has big, important things for you to do. But this envy will eat you alive. It will lead you into bondage for the rest of your life. Won't you please, please stop comparing?"

Friends, envy tugs our hearts toward the Control Girl path. Envy is the opposite of relinquishing control to God. It's the tactic of our enemy who wants to pull us apart and divide us. God wants us to let him be in charge of our differences, embrace who he made us to be, and find peace.

* Do you struggle more with superiority or inferiority? How has Satan used this against you?

* Read James 3:14–4:8 and list out all of the references to Satan's evil regime, along with any references to jealousy, envy, or selfishness.

* Write out a prayer, listing the things God has given you and the things he hasn't. Give gratitude to God and surrender control of this list to him. Draw near to God (James 4:8) and ask him to fill you with peace.

For Meditation: James 4:7

Envy is the opposite of relinquishing control to God. Satan wants to pit me against other people. *God, help me to stop comparing and be free.*

Lesson 3: Thirsty Moms
Read Genesis 30:22–24; 1 Samuel 1

WHEN MY DAUGHTER, Lindsay, was two, my Aunt Joy gave her a white porcelain tea set with little pink roses. Lindsay loved it intensely and had regular tea parties with herself. One day, Aunt Joy stopped over while Lindsay was having "tea." She said, "Oh, how nice. May I have some tea?"

But Lindsay glared at Aunt Joy and quickly began pulling all the cups and saucers in closer, defensively fencing off her tea party with her chubby forearms. Aunt Joy feigned dramatic thirst, and said, "Oh, please? May I have some?" But Lindsay greedily began slurping down thimble-sized cups of water, saying, "No [*slurp*], cause dey are all [*slurp*] mines [*slurp, slurp, slurp*]."

Mothers can sometimes behave like selfish two-year-olds, planning out tea parties for themselves. We pull our children in close like those teacups—a beautiful porcelain set. But rather than serving God with our families and offering up what he first gave us, we defensively fence them off, saying, "No. They're all mine."

Rachel wanted children more than anything in her entire life. But when she finally was blessed with a baby, she named him Joseph, which meant "may he add." She said, "May the LORD add to me another son!" (Gen. 30:24).

Do you hear the thirstiness in Rachel's words? She finally has a baby! But after looking into his sweet little face, she looks up to God, and says, "Yes, and another one too, please." She reminds me of a two-year-old, slurping up what God gave her and reaching for the next one, always thirsty for more. Grasping for control never brings the peaceful satisfaction we imagine it will. It only causes our hearts to chafe against the one who truly *is* in control: God.

God did give Rachel one more baby, but she died during Benjamin's birth. Her life of perpetual thirst was unexpectedly cut short. I can't help but wonder if Rachel would have lived life differently if she had known how little time she had. Would she have worried less about building up her significance and security through her children? I wonder the same about me.

God never designed motherhood to be like a private tea party of self-service. He gave us our "tea sets," not that we might be served, but that we might serve the world with our children. We fill up our kids with love, training, and guidance, and then we extend them graciously, so that others' thirst might be quenched.

Eventually, we give our children away altogether. It's like giving away a beautiful matching tea set, piece by piece. Yes, this can be terribly sad. But my friend Hilma says there is freedom in yielding our children back to God. For her, mothering and grandmothering has been a process of dying. As her kids have grown up, she's had to relinquish them to God. But this has brought her freedom and joy. The other way—with her trying to control them all—made her and them miserable.

Hannah's story told in 1 Samuel is such a beautiful example of the freedom and joy that comes from yielding.

HANNAH'S GIFT

Hannah's circumstance was almost identical to Rachel's. She was one of two wives. Her husband favored her. She couldn't get pregnant. And the other wife was having baby after baby, then cruelly rubbing it in, which was deeply provoking and stressful to Hannah.

At one point, Hannah was so exasperated she couldn't eat. But rather than demanding (as Rachel did) that her husband "do something," Hannah leapt up from the table and ran to the temple to seek God.

Apparently she was all blubbery and snotty, not caring what anyone thought, because the priest supposed she was drunk. But Hannah said, "No, my lord, I am a woman troubled in spirit. . . . I have been pouring out my soul before the LORD" (1 Sam. 1:15).

After Hannah explained her situation, the kindly priest told her to go home, trust God, and not worry anymore. And remarkably, Hannah did exactly that. She returned to the table with her sadness lifted and desperation gone. God had filled her with hope.

About a year later, Hannah's arms were finally full. But rather than looking into that sweet, little face and demanding another baby, Hannah did something entirely different. She brought her little boy to live with the priest and serve at the temple, saying, "As long as he lives, he is lent to the LORD" (1 Sam. 1:28).

Hannah trusted intensely. She sweetly surrendered control to God.

In contrast, Rachel yearned intensely. She was a Control Girl, always thirsty for more.

AMY'S SACRIFICE

Fear is often what keeps us from relinquishing control. My friend Amy is one of the sweetest, kindest people I know. For Amy, fear has always been a struggle. When our kids were little, she worried about things I never considered worrying about. And the fear that trumped all was losing one of her kids. If that ever happened, Amy supposed she would spend the rest of her life in a fetal position.

But Amy did lose one of her children. Just a few months ago, she lost her precious, spunky, tree-climbing, artistic, thirteen-year-old Becca. When I talked to Amy just after they learned of the cancer, she told me, "I finally realize how silly I've been. God has seen fit to entrust these five beautiful children to me, but I can't entrust them back to him?"

Amy spent a year entrusting Becca, little by little, back to God. And then she had to give her up completely. But at the funeral, Amy was at her absolute best. Gone was the fear, and shining out from her was such faith and hope that I have scarcely ever seen. Yes, her sacrifice was horrific and deeply painful. But Amy, like Hannah, had poured out her grief to the Lord. She had lent dear Becca back to him.

Rachel's story shows us that we cannot control the future. We could spend our whole lives fencing off what is "ours," slurping up whatever we get our hands on, and still die as thirsty Control Girls. Or we can be like Hannah and pour out the pain in our souls—all blubbery, snotty, and uninhibited—before God. When we say, "The LORD is my chosen portion and my cup; you hold my lot" (Ps. 16:5), we find comfort, freedom, and peace.

❀   Who are you more like, Hannah or Rachel? In what ways are you
    like her?

❀   What are you continually thirsty for? Is there a chance you might
    always be thirsty for more? What can you learn from Rachel?

❀   How is fear keeping you from relinquishing control of a situation
    or person you love?

❀   Read 1 Samuel 1:24–28. What is God calling you to "lend" back to
    him, as Hannah did? Or how have you already found freedom by
    doing so?

For Meditation: Psalm 16:5

When I fearfully try to pull in and fence off what is mine, my thirst
is never quenched. *Father, I want to know the freedom of entrusting my life and
my children back to you.*

Lesson 4: A Chunky Board Book
Read Genesis 50:17–20; Romans 8:28–31

ONCE, WHEN MY youngest was out riding his tricycle on the sidewalk, we stopped to talk with some people walking by. They asked him where he lived, and he pointed to our house, saying, "I libs over dere wiff my two kids."

I laughed at the way he referred to his siblings and completely omitted his dad and me, who also "libs over dere," and happen to pay the mortgage, cut up his meat for him, and wrap him in a warm towel after his bath.

It was funny then. But as an adult, if our son still omits us from his life story, it won't be nearly as funny. To some degree, we're all tempted to tell our stories the way a three-year-old would, failing to recognize the bigger, broader story about a Father who provides and cares for us. It's his story that we are folded into.

BOARD BOOK VERSION

As a Control Girl, I'm particularly guilty of this. I have my fingers clamped onto a "chunky board book" version of my life story that I happen to like. It's brightly illustrated and has a simple plot that never thickens with conflict, suffering, or pain. And the book is durable. You can't bend its pages. If you open it up, you'll see that I'm the central character, and if you read it, you'll get to the Happy Ending in three minutes flat.

I think Rachel wanted a chunky board book version for her story too. She wanted a sweet, straightforward story line where she was the heroine-princess who had lots of babies.

The end.

But God had something far more grandiose in mind for Rachel. He was writing a sweeping story line, full of staggering prophecies, swelling love stories, shocking betrayals, and gut-wrenching battles, all with Rachel's family at the center. The breathtaking plot, which spanned centuries, was to culminate with a conquering King of the Ages.

Rachel got to be part of something truly great, but she refused to see it. She didn't want God's 30,000-foot view of her family. Rachel remained completely detached from God's bigger, richer plot. Instead, she engrossed herself in the rivalry with her sister, fixated on filling her side of the family tree.

Rachel lived the life of a Control Girl.

As she stressed and fretted over her family's little maternity ward, Rachel was oblivious to the fact that God had just birthed the nation of Israel. Rachel's family would become God's people, making his name famous in all the earth. Rachel's own baby, Joseph, would become a foreign ruler, whose powerful protection would save his extended family from being obliterated by famine.

"If you knew you were going to be the mother of Joseph, would that be enough for you?" This is the question I want to ask Rachel, as she paces beside her empty crib. She didn't know, of course. But from where I sit, it seems silly that the mother of Joseph—the man whose fame has spanned the ages—would be fretting about a life of obscurity.

With beauty and intrigue, the Bible uses Joseph's story to show God powerfully working behind the scenes of trouble or difficulty to weave together a Happy Ending that doesn't seem so happy at the moment. Joseph—Rachel's boy—rose above betrayal and injustice and famously said, "You meant evil against me, but God meant it for good" (Gen. 50:20).

THE AUTHOR OF ALL

If Rachel could have a warped perspective on her life, surely we can too. When God says he's working all things together for good (Rom. 8:28), he isn't talking about our chunky board book versions of the story. God has a perspective of "all things" that spans both forward and backward as far as you can go. Because of his breadth of wisdom, his ability to orchestrate good isn't even fathomable to us.

God is like a brilliant novelist, masterfully twisting together a billion plotlines at once and skillfully moving each part of the story line toward a conclusion that will be richly satisfying for all. God has an astounding, thrilling, ever-swelling ending already worked out, and he's threading the details of it through each of our lives.

This is God's story—about him and his family, not me and mine. But I still get to be part of the story. Psalm 139:16 says, "In your book were written, every one of them, the days that were formed for me." Like Rachel, the tiny paragraphs of my life are folded into God's colossal, exquisite story.

Recognizing this makes my chunky board book heroine goal seem rather ridiculous. My simple endings are so unsatisfying compared to what God is writing. When I see that God's plot underlines every part of my story, I have less to worry about and less to control. Even if my adult child stops going to church, or I find a lump under my skin, or I face an unexpected financial crisis, I know that the end is still being written. **God's pen is still poised above the details of my life.**

SOMETHING BETTER

Earlier I mentioned Amy, who lost her thirteen-year-old, Becca, to cancer. In one of the updates that Amy sent out, she wrote, "We specifically hope that . . . God would refine us and glorify himself through this time and through Becca's living. Please pray that we would be at peace with God's will if he has something better for us."

Something better? Better than Becca living? Do you hear the deep surrender and faith in Amy's words? Do you see how God was already at work, refining my dear, sweet friend, and glorifying himself through her faith?

This is God's goal every single time he withholds the thing I am begging for or stomping my foot over. God is doing something good from a 30,000-foot perspective. He is intertwining scenes with more complexity than I could fathom and fashioning the whole story for his purposes. And the Happy Ending God is writing for my family is richer, bigger, and far more satisfying than anything I could ever write for myself.

❀ In two sentences, summarize your chunky board book version of a happy ending.

❀ How will you make your life story more about God and less about you, in the next month?

❀ What difficulties has God brought your way? Do you trust that God is working these things together for good, even if you can't see how?

For Meditation: Romans 8:28

My life is a story about God and his family, not me and mine. *God, I believe that your pen is poised over the details of my life, and that you are writing a more satisfying ending than I can even fathom.*

Rachel's Unhappy Ending

RACHEL NEVER SAW beyond her own, small self, which makes her story rather sad and disheartening. She spent her whole life playing tug-of-war with her sister, trying to control her end of the rope, never realizing that God was already doing something good.

Rachel's son, Joseph, is the poster child for the concept of God being in control. He said famously, "You meant evil against me, but God meant it for good." But I doubt Joseph learned this perspective from his mama.

Rachel was shortsighted. She fixated on filling her side of the family tree and never caught sight of the bigger story God was writing.

Chapter Eight
Miriam: Taking the Lead

❀ ONCE UPON a time, in the land of Egypt, there was a little slave girl named Miriam who had the markings of a great leader. She befriended Pharoah's daughter, saved her baby brother from death, and forever changed the destiny of her people.

But this fiercely protective big sister grew into a controlling big sister who needed to be taught a lesson. Miriam's story rings out as a warning to strong women who lead God's people, but first must learn to be led by him.

Lesson 1: Gifted to Lead
Read Exodus 2:1–10; 15:19–21

MY FRIEND CHRIS came home one evening to find his seven-year-old daughter, Allie, in a tent with her two younger brothers. She was giving them the new rules for their "town," and had even posted them:

1. No steeling
2. No kiling
3. No being mean
4. No cheeding
5. No choices

Allie's last rule (a Control Girl classic) is my favorite. It's not surprising that she is now in law school. I've always known she was destined for greatness. Even this glimpse into her childhood shows Allie's leadership gifts surfacing behind the tent flap.

Miriam was probably about Allie's age when she watched over her baby brother in the basket. Like Allie, Miriam's leadership skills were already surfacing. She must have been a responsible, trustworthy little girl to be included in her mother's daring scheme to defy Pharaoh's ruling.

Pharaoh had demanded that all boy babies be thrown into the Nile. Rather than committing such an atrocity, Moses's mother made a waterproof basket and hid him in the reeds near the riverbank, stationing big sister Miriam nearby to watch. Since the princess came to bathe near their hiding spot, it must not have been highly frequented by men. Smart mama, right? And she had an equally smart little girl.

Miriam, looking on while the princess discovered her brother's hiding spot, was impressively perceptive and wise. After she saw the princess melt with compassion, Miriam waited for just the right moment to boldly step out and offer, "Shall I go and call you a nurse from the Hebrew women to nurse the child for you?" (Exod. 2:7).

Notice how Miriam didn't freeze in fear or holler for them to get their hands off her brother. She didn't say, "Yeah, my mom hid him there because your evil father is trying to kill him." As she capitalized on the moment, Miriam was discerning enough to keep the princess's perspective in mind and astute enough to conceal her own identity. She presented herself as a little girl who just happened to be there, offering her services.

Because of Miriam, Moses was saved from Pharaoh's plot to annihilate any boys who might grow up to defy him. Ironically, Pharaoh's fears were justified, for by saving *this* baby, a little girl has just begun to unravel Pharaoh's slave-fortified empire.

WOMEN IN LEADERSHIP

Baby Moses was eventually taken to live with Pharaoh, the enslaver of Miriam's people. Surely such irony wasn't wasted on such a perceptive big sister. God had put their ancestor, Joseph, in Pharaoh's palace, to deliver his people. Could God be planning to do the same with her baby brother? God had promised Abraham that, after four hundred years of enslavement, Israel would be freed (Gen. 15:13–14). Would God use Moses to leverage their freedom?

I'll bet Miriam had these questions, just as surely as you and I wonder if we'll see Jesus return. And then, when her brother finally stood up to Pharaoh and said, "Let my people go!" how Miriam's heart must have swelled with pride. Then, before her very eyes, the Red Sea parted beneath her brother's staff.

On the banks of the Red Sea that next morning, with Pharaoh's horses and riders washing up behind her, Miriam took her tambourine and led the women of Israel in dancing and song. They were delivered! It was a pinnacle moment of Miriam's devotion to God.

CONTROL GIRLS IN LEADERSHIP

The Bible calls Miriam a prophetess, which means she wasn't shy about speaking out for the Lord. Her gifts for leadership were obvious to all. She got to play the pivotal role of inspiring God's people to worship and honor him during one of Israel's most celebrated events. The parting of the Red Sea is raised like a banner throughout Scripture, saying, "This is who God is."

But Miriam's story shows how quickly we can fall. Just a year later, Miriam stepped out, not as a God-honoring leader, but as a Control Girl. In the wilderness, she undermined Moses's authority and campaigned for more power among God's people.

No longer was Miriam out in front, raising a banner that declared who God is. She makes us raise our eyebrows and ask, "Just who do you think *you* are?" This is a grave risk for women in leadership, especially in the church. And apparently—since Miriam was probably in her nineties at this point—it's a problem we don't outgrow. God's response to Miriam shows that he does not take arrogant, self-promoting attitudes lightly; nor should we.

A Controlling Leader

Zelda is a woman clearly gifted for leadership. Over past decades, a women's Bible study in her church has blossomed under Zelda's care. She has been profoundly used by God to lead women to freedom in Christ.

The leaders serving under Zelda, however, were not experiencing freedom. If ever a leader wanted to change the slightest thing—like shifting prayer requests to the beginning or using a different Bible translation—Zelda bristled immediately and defended her proven methods. As a result, her leaders began taking their innovative creativity either underground or out the door.

One day, Angelina was at church helping with setup for a ladies' event when everything came to a screeching halt. A very angry Zelda marched over, got six inches from Angelina's face, and screamed in shrill tones, "That is *not* where I told you to put the punch!"

The other women who were helping thought maybe Angelina had *thrown* a punch, given the anger in Zelda's tone! The most remarkable thing about it, however, was how Zelda never broke stride. She never apologized. She never checked on Angelina's feelings. She just kept bustling around, doing "ministry." For her, it had been a nonevent.

Zelda, just who do you think you are? we wonder. It's a question each ministry leader needs to ask herself. Yes, Zelda's personal formula for ministry has produced spiritual fruit; there's no questioning that. What is questionable, however, is the focus of her ministry. It had become a reflection of Zelda, not God. And her passion for God's name had begun to overlap with a passion for her own name.

Whenever we make God's ministry into *our* ministry, we will take both control and credit. And according to God, neither belongs to us.

From her small beginning as a slave girl watching over her brother, to her dance on the banks of the Red Sea, Miriam was gifted and positioned to serve God in spectacular ways. God positions us to do great things for him too. However, any ministry we are privileged to participate in is not our own; it all belongs to God.

- Are you gifted for leadership? How did these gifts surface? How has God particularly positioned you to serve him?

- Have you made God's ministry into your ministry? How can you release control?

- Ask yourself, *Who do you think you are?* How can you make things right with those you may have hurt?

For Meditation: 2 Timothy 2:24

When I make God's ministry into my ministry, I take credit and control, which both belong to God. *God, I know that my gifts are from you. May my service lift up your name, not mine.*

Lesson 2: In the Lead
Read Numbers 12:1–8

BOTH MEN AND women can be controlling leaders, but women tend to do it a bit differently. We control by leveraging the relationships and networks we're so good at building. We use our people skills to get what we want. On the flip side, when our idea gets shot down or our concern is disregarded, we often take it more personally than men do. Especially at church.

An investment at church represents an offering to God! Laying a gift on the altar is deeply personal and meaningful. So it stings when the deacons vote to discontinue the ministry we founded. It's personal when only six people sign up for the retreat we planned. It hurts when the committee doesn't need our help this year.

For Miriam, ministry was personal as well. She felt rejected, slighted, and marginalized by her brother Moses. But she should not have responded by stirring up dissention among God's people.

Let's ask God to show us any similar patterns in ourselves as we consider three aspects of Miriam's sin: hidden agendas, verbal bullets, and recruiting supporters.

HIDDEN AGENDAS

We women are especially good at camouflaging our true agendas. Suppose a committee member says, "I think the younger gals will want to be in a group together," but she's privately thinking, "Don't put them with me. I can't stand their silly conversations or their crying newborns." See how she raises a smoke screen to keep her bias out of the conversation?

That's what Miriam did when she brought up the ethnicity of Moses's wife, who was not Jewish. Apparently Miriam had a problem with that. But God didn't, since he vehemently defended Moses. Regardless, Miriam is just camouflaging her true agenda.

Control Girls are often less than direct. We raise concerns, but keep our selfish motives to ourselves. Yet, to God, nothing is hidden. He sees our murky hearts with perfect clarity. He revealed Miriam's selfish ambition, and he'll do the same for us if we invite him to.

🏵 What or who are you most passionately resisting or taking a stand against?

🏵 Invite the Spirit to probe your motives and reveal truth to you. Are you harboring any pride, jealousy, arrogance, fear, or stubbornness that contributes to the conflict?

🏵 Confess your hidden motives to God, and ask him to change your heart and give you supernatural peace, humility, and grace.

VERBAL BULLETS

The story about Miriam and Aaron speaking against Moses in Numbers 12 uses feminine singular verbs. In other words, Aaron was passive (just like he was about the golden calf in Exodus 32). Miriam is the one attacking Moses, and she's using words as her weapon of choice.[1]

In today's world, it takes just a click to shoot verbal bullets or spray inflammatory shrapnel. But even without social media, Miriam harnessed the power of social networking to rally supporters and undermine authority.

The Hebrew grammar in this passage gives the impression that this is not a one-time event. Miriam's challenge is ongoing and with swelling intensity. She's getting louder and more forceful. She's like the agitated lid over a boiling pot of water, rattling and spitting steam. She's becoming *more* convinced she's right, and she will not let it go, which is typical for Control Girls.[2]

Women tend to process conflict over time. A guy might want one intense discussion with the decision maker, but a woman craves multiple conversations, often with everyone *but* the decision maker. We justify gossip because we "just need to talk it through." We become deeply unsettled for days or months, and everyone knows it—including God.[3]

As Miriam spewed, she failed to recognize how closely God was listening in. And she didn't consider how far her voice traveled as a leader in Israel. As Miriam was foolishly unleashing her words in public, God cut in. Numbers 12:4 says, "Suddenly, the LORD said to Moses and to Aaron and Miriam, 'Come out, you three, to the tent of meeting.'" And from this point on in Scripture, Miriam's voice is silent.

Ladies, let's not be rattling lids that God must silence. We each influence someone and **the farther our voice travels, the more accountable we are to God**.

⚜ How does Miriam's story illustrate James 3:1–18? How about your story?

⚜ What do you talk about incessantly and refuse to let go of? Consider "muting" yourself on this issue for a time and turning exclusively to God.

⚜ How have you communicated—either in person or using an electronic device—in an inflammatory, undermining, or divisive way? How can you make this right?

RECRUITING SUPPORTERS

Rather than statements, notice that Miriam uses questions to invoke a response. She asks, "Has the LORD indeed spoken only through Moses?" (Num. 12:2). She asks it repeatedly, which means she's not really looking for an answer, but a reaction. She wants to recruit supporters who will affirm her indignation.

Women tend to process frustration—especially toward leadership—in social groups. We find gratification in framing an issue so that our girlfriends say, "What in the world? Are you serious?" Their solidarity gives us a regained sense of control.

We also use emotions to solicit support. One pastor told me about a woman on his team who starts crying whenever she is challenged. "That disarms most men," he said. "And she's very strong, so most of the time her tears are intentional, and she knows it." This pastor also mentioned the power of the female pout. He said, "Again, this disarms most men. We are fixers by nature."

But whether we're lobbying to men or women, it's important to note that the people of God aren't ruled by democracy; we are led by God. No matter how many people we recruit, by raising opposition against church leaders, we raise opposition against God.[4]

Now, is it ever appropriate to call a leader into question? Absolutely. You can find instructions for that in Matthew 18. What you won't find is permission to incite a protest in the church. When Miriam did this, God took it personally. He responded with a question of his own: "Why then were you not afraid to speak against my servant Moses?" (Num. 12:8).

God wanted Miriam to remember her place. She was once a slave girl, whom God chose to rescue and then positioned for his name's sake. And that's who we are too. Once slaves to sin, God led us from captivity and positioned us to do great things for him. But he wants us to remember our place. Like Israel following the cloud of God's presence in the wilderness, we would be lost without God. He leads our leaders. With them, we follow God.

Friends, let's be extremely cautious about challenging church leadership publicly or regularly. When we've been personally hurt or offended by leadership, we want to careen down the Control Girl path, recruiting whoever will endorse our frustration. But God wants us to handle pain and frustration the right way, by turning *to* the Lord, not against him.

❀ How have you taken a stand against your church leaders, and recruited support for your viewpoint? Write out a plan to make this right.

❀ List out any frustrations you have with church leaders God has put in place. Now pray about each item, and give control to God, asking him to lead your leaders.

❀ Read Hebrews 13:17 and list both instructions and reasons given.

For Meditation: Hebrews 13:17

I would be lost without God's direction, and he uses my leaders to give it. *God, I don't want to be a "rattling lid" that you must silence. Help me bring my frustrations directly to you.*

Lesson 3: Sharing Leadership
Read Numbers 11:4–35

MIRIAM'S STRONG REACTION against Moses wasn't a random, isolated event. In the last lesson, we pieced apart what Miriam did; in this lesson we'll look at *why*, by backing up a chapter to Numbers 11.

When sorting through our control issues, it's helpful to get our bearings and ask, "What am I trying to control? What do I feel like I'm losing control of?" It's also helpful to ask, "What does God want me to surrender? What is he teaching me?"

GRAVES OF CRAVING

There are two significant stories layered throughout Numbers 11. The first one opens with pathetic groans rising up from all over the sprawling clans of Israel. The people moaned in unison about how sick of manna they were. They wanted meat.

So God sent a swarm of quail. Then, while they gorged themselves, people became extremely ill. Many died. Rather than digging into meat, they dug graves for their family members and friends. It was utterly devastating.

Funerals are the ultimate cord-dangling moments of life. God used these mass graves to help his people gain perspective and ready them for what was just ahead—taking the Promised Land as their own. As the cloud of God's presence led the people away from the Graves of Craving, God wanted them to somberly leave behind their sinful complaining and follow him with new, wholehearted surrender.

It's remarkable that Miriam did not. The mass funeral seems to have had no effect on her. With complete disregard for God's lesson on complaining, Miriam fires up her jaw to file complaints about something new: Moses's leadership.

It's preposterous. And yet, it's so possible. **As disoriented, hardened leaders, we can convince ourselves that God's lessons are for everyone except ourselves.**

Once, on the way to a speaking engagement, I realized that I had been sinfully ignoring the very truth I planned to speak on. With deep conviction, I pulled off the road and confessed my willful resistance to the Lord. Then I pulled into a nearby store for some new mascara to replace what was now streaming down my face.

I would far rather approach a group of ladies with patched makeup and a contrite spirit than with a false sense that the lesson is not for me. It's *always* for me.

If only Miriam had heeded God's personal lesson on complaining for her back at the Graves of Craving, she could have prevented the biggest mistake of her life. But I have a hunch that rather than turning her attention to God's admonitions, Miriam was absorbed and distracted by the *other* story unfolding in Numbers 11, especially since it involved the very thing Miriam craved—leadership recognition.

Newbie Leaders

Back when the people began groaning about the manna, Moses went moaning to God. So God appointed seventy new spiritual leaders to share Moses's burdens. As the new leaders gathered for orientation at the congregational tent, for some unknown reason, two of the seventy stayed back at the camp.

These two began prophesying and making quite a stir. Someone came running with a report, and Joshua urged Moses to make the two prophets stop. "But Moses said to him, 'Are you jealous for my sake? Would that all the LORD's people were prophets, that the LORD would put his Spirit on them!'" (Num. 11:29).

Rather than feeling threatened, Moses welcomes these new leaders. Rather than protecting his notoriety, Moses wishes there could be more prophets. Moses in his humility holds stark contrast to Miriam, arrogantly defending her turf in Numbers 12. As she reminds everyone that Moses isn't the *only* one who hears from God, perhaps it's because she—unlike Moses—*does* feel threatened and displaced by the new leaders. Maybe she's been working the new organizational chart out in her head, and she's wondering if her prominence has to be split seventy new ways. Surely, she belongs up a tier with Moses and Aaron, doesn't she?

The Bible does not say whether the seventy newbie leaders contributed to Miriam's agitation, but knowing my own heart struggles, I can certainly imagine this being the case. It's really hard to be like Moses and say, "If only all of God's people had my gifts and could do what I do best." It's hard to not feel threatened by others who do what I do . . . and do it better. It's especially hard when they are given more responsibility than me. Or they attract more followers. Or get more "likes" on Facebook.

NAGGING QUESTIONS

Once, another speaker and I showed up the same day, planning to speak to a ladies' group. They solved the mix-up by letting us both present in different rooms and having the ladies choose which topic they wanted to hear—my heavy, spiritual topic, or the lighthearted, fun one down the hall.

As you can imagine, about seventy-five percent of the women went down the hall.

I called my friend Jill that afternoon and told her how much it hurt to see the women flocking to the other room. There was a bit of judgment in my tone too, as I complained that women today would rather be entertained than be challenged with truth.

Jill said, "Well, I might have gone to that other room too."

It wasn't what I wanted to hear, but I knew my friend was trying to help me. She wanted me to see that even as one of my biggest fans, she might have chosen the other topic. But that didn't mean that she loved me less or thought I had nothing to contribute. It just meant she liked the other topic more.

Ladies in ministry often have these nagging questions lurking beneath the surface: Am I needed? Is God using me? Am I qualified for this role? Is this really what God wants me to do?

We try to quell our fears by collecting compliments. Or recording attendance. Or amassing followers. And then, when it becomes obvious that some fresh, new leader is displacing us, we feel threatened, deflated, and agitated.

Oh, friends, this is absolutely crucial to our surrender process. So many women in the church are turf-oriented and defensive. They are Control Girls in leadership. But as with Miriam, God wants us to surrender our cravings for honor and recognition to him.

God wants us to come regularly to receive our individual assignment and serving platter from him. Will we feed thousands or just one? Will we serve with notoriety or anonymity? Will we lead for a long time or just a moment? These are all answered by the One who leads *us*.

As Miriam's story shows, we must fix our passion on *being* a follower of God, not *gathering* followers for ourselves. So instead of turning around to obsess over how many followers we have, God invites us to face forward and peacefully follow him.

- ❀ Write a summary of what God has done in your life this past year. Is there a lesson you have been rigidly immune to?

- ❀ Do you feel threatened by others who do what you do? How can you surrender your "turf" to God, rather than defending it?

- ❀ What's one tangible way you can face forward and focus on following God rather than gathering followers?

- ❀ What has God put on your "serving platter"? Are you content with this? Write out a prayer, surrendering your ministry cravings to God.

For Meditation: Philippians 2:3–7

Rather than defending my turf or obsessing over how many followers I have, I will face forward and follow God. *Lord, I surrender my cravings for honor and recognition to you.*

Lesson 4: Healing a Control Girl
Read Numbers 12

MIRIAM WAS RIGHT in the middle of grabbing honor for herself when God interrupted. His voice slapped like thunder across the camp, summoning Miriam and her brothers for an immediate meeting. God swiftly set things straight, and then the cloud of his presence lifted to dramatically reveal Miriam, white with leprosy. God had brought the decay in Miriam's heart to the surface so it could be dealt with.

Correction is pivotal for Control Girls. We can either willfully persist in our sin or surrender to God. Miriam's story provides three ways to yield to God during times of correction: involve others, be humbled, and do the sideline shuffle.

INVOLVE OTHERS

Picture this: Miriam was right in the middle of challenging Moses's direct line to God, arguing that she also talks to God just like Moses does. Then, minutes later, with half-eaten skin, Miriam must concede that she's not as self-sufficient as she thought. She needs Moses to talk to God for her. So Moses prays, and Miriam is healed.

God could have dealt with Miriam one-on-one, but he involved her brothers in both her correction and her healing. We need to adopt Miriam's new vantage point. Self-sufficiency is a façade. We are *not* OK on our own. God has meticulously placed us into the body of Christ. We need each other, especially for correction.

This is difficult for Control Girl leaders. It takes extra humility for a women's ministry director to ask for help with an addiction or a Bible study leader to ask for counsel about anxiety. But God designed all of us—leaders included—to be interdependent.

To resist involving others, or to resist asking for prayer or help, is pure arrogance. It's as foolish as Miriam—half-eaten with leprosy—would have been to refuse Moses's prayers. Control Girl, if God has surfaced some decay of your heart, don't be foolish and try to handle it on your own. Invite other godly people to be part of your healing.

BE HUMBLED

I often want to immediately retract my kids' consequences the moment they show a smidgen of repentance, but my husband insists we don't. The humbling process isn't easy or quick. It requires consequences that hurt for a while. Being humbled involves many tears and a sick feeling that lingers in your gut.

God gave Miriam a seven-day shunning. This was drastically humbling for such a prominent leader. She was ostracized. The entire nation was at a standstill, waiting. It was especially dramatic given the way God intervened—as newsworthy as a politician's arrest during a campaign speech, followed by a police escort to jail.

God supports humble leaders like Moses (Num. 12:3). But when a leader is willful and self-promoting, God won't hold back. He uses whatever means necessary to cut away our thick calluses of arrogance and pride. Yet, **when God shaves the controlling parts from our hearts, he is being good and kind**. I've learned this by experience.

Awhile back, a group I helped lead was divided over a conflict, and I had been willfully persistent in my viewpoint. As I solicited validation from other leaders and carefully examined Scripture, I became increasingly convinced that I was right.

The situation escalated, and we set a meeting to talk things through. To prepare, I got in contact with Annette, who was part of a mediation ministry, hoping she could give guidance on diffusing our group's tension. As Annette and I spoke, something unexpected happened. Empowered by God's Spirit, Annette gently helped me see the error of my ways.

I realized I had been far more consumed with doing and being right than with loving and serving the people in my group. After speaking with Annette, I went straight to God's Word and was stunned at what I found there. It seemed that every passage I turned to revealed with fresh clarity how wrong I had been. I spent several hours, with hot tears dropping onto the pages of my Bible, crying out in repentance to God. I tore up the notes I had prepared for the meeting and instead wrote out a letter asking my group to forgive me. And they did.

This was one of the sweetest experiences of my entire Christian life. Yes, God had been sharply corrective. Yes, it was utterly humbling. But as God shaved away the ugly, sinful parts of my controlling heart, I felt free to love and to grow. I also had new peace, because I wasn't urgently trying to control our group's outcomes; I was content to let God do that.

Like Miriam, we Control Girls are often completely oblivious to our own contributions to conflict. But God is faithful to shave away the patches of arrogance from our hearts, allowing us to pursue true greatness through serving others, not ourselves.

DO THE SIDELINE SHUFFLE

God could have kept Miriam's correction private, but he made it public. Perhaps the people didn't see her leprosy, but everyone knew about her being escorted outside the camp.

Public dismissal to the sidelines is incredibly difficult for a Control Girl. It's hard to control anything from over there, including our reputations. Yet God often uses the sidelines to heal our controlling hearts. He sends us there not to push us away, but to pull us closer to him. God wants us to have the space to be still, reshuffle our priorities, and refocus on him.

Ashley asked me to meet her for coffee just after she had been sidelined from ministry. She felt ashamed, frustrated, and devastated over what had happened. But when I asked what God was teaching her, Ashley said she had been too distraught to open her Bible.

I said, "Oh, Ashley! That's what this time is *for*. By pausing your ministry, God is inviting you to draw near." I told Ashley the next time we met I wanted to hear about the verses God had used to comfort, guide, or correct her.

But two weeks later, Ashley still had not opened God's Word. She reiterated her grief over being sidelined and how stuck she felt. I gave

Ashley the same assignment again, saying earnestly, "Ashley, this is what you need. This will make the 'sideline' worth it!"

The third time we met, Ashley still hadn't sought the Lord in his Word.

Control Girl, if God has sidelined you and kept you from stubbornly pushing your agenda, this is his grace in your life. It means that he is refusing to let you trudge off down the path of the ugly Control Girl. He loves you enough to sacrifice whatever ministry contributions you might be making, in order to draw you back, closer to him.

❀ How has God brought the decay of your heart to the surface? How will you involve others in your healing?

❀ Ask God to shave away any calluses of arrogance and pride. Watch for his correction through your circumstances, other believers, and his Word.

❀ What have you been sidelined from? How has God used this to draw you near?

For Meditation: Isaiah 30:15

God wants to bring my sin to the surface so he can shave off my calluses of pride. *God, thank you that you use the sidelines in life to pull me closer, not push me away.*

Miriam's Happy Ending

GOD WAS WILLING to stall his people for one week as they waited for Miriam outside the camp. Obviously, he thought she was worth it. And when Miriam rejoined God's people, I can't help but believe that the decay had been removed from both her skin and her heart.

Miriam's story has a lesson for Control Girls of all ages. If we are gifted to take the lead, we must be careful to first follow God's lead.

Chapter Nine
Control Girl to Jesus Girl

ONE AFTERNOON, after waking up from a nap, my toddler, Cade, sat dazed at the top of our stairs. I came around the corner just in time to see his older brother come from behind and give him a big shove! By some miracle, Cade shot his pudgy little hand out and caught the railing, keeping himself from tumbling down the stairs. He hung there, stunned, like a little monkey.

"Cole!" I said incredulously, swooping Cade into my arms. "*Why* did you try to push your baby brother down the stairs?"

"Oh, I wasn't trying to hurt him, Mommy," Cole said. "But he was sitting on my fruit of the Spirit paper from Sunday school."

The irony is funny now, but it wasn't then.

Many Control Girls treat the Holy Spirit like Cole did. We learn about the Holy Spirit in church, but don't expect him to change our behavior that very afternoon. We *say* God is in control, and then we shove people aside and selfishly forge ahead with our personal agendas.

If we lived at the time Jesus rose from the dead, we would have witnessed a dramatic transformation in the people who first received the Holy Spirit. First they were timidly hiding behind locked doors. Then they were boldly preaching on the temple's porch. Peter went from denying Jesus to proclaiming him. Paul went from murdering Christians to discipling them. Individuals who had shouted, "Crucify him!" made Jesus their Lord.

What made the difference? God's Spirit. And since this same Spirit is living in us, we should expect dramatic transformation in our own lives. Second Corinthians 3:18 says that the Spirit is transforming each of us to make us look more and more like Jesus. He turns us from Control Girls into Jesus Girls.

Lesson 1: Reverse of the Curse
Read 2 Corinthians 3:17–18; Galatians 5:22–26

SOMETIMES I'M SKEPTICAL when I hear about the Spirit's power to change me. I've been a Control Girl for a long time. I don't like this about myself, but sometimes I secretly wonder, *Can the Holy Spirit truly make a difference in my life?*

It can be equally disheartening to hear about others. Often, when someone tells me about the controlling woman in her life, I'll ask, "Is she a Christian?" The answer is commonly yes—she loves God and is committed to him. *Then why isn't God changing her?* I wonder.

Control Girls seem particularly resistant to change. It's a problem that doesn't go away on its own and usually gets worse with age. But it makes sense, when you consider that change comes from yielding control to God, which is exactly what Control Girls don't do. We posture ourselves to *take* control. Rather than yielding to God, we cave in to ourselves and that desire we have to control. Transformation comes from doing the opposite of this.

Ephesians 5:18 says, "And do not get drunk with wine . . . but be filled with the Spirit." A person filled with alcohol has less control than usual, because she's under its influence. And a person filled with God's Spirit has less control than usual, because she's under *his* influence. She does things that are uncharacteristic and people notice. Rather than trying to control everything, she's giving control to God.

Did you realize that the Control Girls of the Old Testament didn't have the Spirit to guide them? No wonder they stumbled as they did. We, on the other hand, have the Spirit inside of us, showing us which way to go. To fill ourselves with the Spirit, we fill our minds and hearts with his influence. We read the Bible. We listen for his voice in prayer. We put media and other influences on mute so we can hear his voice more clearly.

John 16:13 says that the Spirit comes to "guide [us] into all the truth." So, as we fill ourselves with the Spirit's influence, he guides us away from the lie that we have to take control and make everything turn out right. That's the Control Girl path. It makes us angry and fearful, remember? God's way is filled with peace, joy, and security. It's the way we've been ultimately trying to find all along. But we only find it when we yield to the Spirit.

We yield. He guides. And step by step, as we walk this new path, we're transformed from Control Girls to Jesus Girls.

BIG ARROWS

Think of the Spirit's guidance as arrows placed in your path to give direction in life. Sometimes the arrows offer dramatic course correction. I call these "Big Arrow" experiences. You were headed one way, and God interrupted. Your trajectory shifted notably.

Turning to Christ for salvation is a Big Arrow experience. You couldn't turn to Jesus if the Spirit hadn't opened your eyes and drawn your heart. You might also recall other Big Arrow shifts on your Christian journey. Maybe the Holy Spirit compelled you to turn from a certain career path, relationship, or dream. Or perhaps he asked you to sacrifice something dear. No doubt, these Big Arrow seasons were marked by pain, but perhaps you also think back on them with great joy, knowing that the Spirit shifted your internal compass and pointed you to Jesus.

When the Spirit is at work, we *want* to change directions. But remember that surrender isn't passive or inactive. Giving God control often involves straining against myself. As I yield to the Spirit, my blood pressure is up and my heart rate is high. Like Hagar, when she turned back after running away. Or Sarah, when she opened her heart to hoping for a baby at age eighty-nine. Or Rebekah, when she left home to marry a stranger.

These were moments of high-octane surrender, each prompted by giving God control. Our direction in life is largely determined by whether we yield to the Big Arrows that God's Spirit lays out for us.

SMALL ARROWS

While it would be wrong to minimize the Big Arrows, I believe "Small Arrows" are even more transformational. Here's why: It's possible to yield to God on Big Arrows, spaced out by decades, and then live the rest of our lives as Control Girls. It's possible to give God control of big decisions and then ignore his Spirit for the small ones. It's possible to make Jesus our King and then live like a Control Girl queen.

I'm sure we all know somebody like that.

Today, right now, we are becoming the women we will someday be. Little by little, our hearts are heading in one direction or the other. On a moment-by-moment basis, we either gratify our craving for control or we surrender control to God. Either we say yes to ourselves or we say yes to the Spirit. We can't do both. That would be like trying to follow arrows pointing in opposite directions.

It's great to throw my head back and say, "God, take control of my life!" But if I only give God control of the indefinite future and never the next five minutes, I won't be transformed. Change happens gradually, during the small moments of the day. Like when I'm dying inside because the coach still has my son on the bench. Or I'm fuming as I get into bed because my husband is still watching TV. Or I'm in turmoil for the fifteenth time today, wondering if the cancer has spread.

Galatians 5:25 says, "If we live by the Spirit, let us also keep in step with the Spirit." Our transformation from Control Girls to Jesus Girls is a series of small steps, each influenced by the Spirit. As we yield to the Spirit's Small Arrows, our hearts are trained. The general direction of our lives becomes Spirit-led.

You've now studied seven Control Girls in the Bible, all of whom responded to God in various ways. Now it's your turn. How will you respond? Of course, I can't do the Spirit's job of laying down arrows in your path, but for our remaining lessons, I've chosen four Small Arrows that Control Girls tend to ignore. Do you want to be transformed from Control Girl to Jesus Girl? Then use these last pages to listen to the Spirit as he invites you to:

1. Tame your tongue
2. Cap the red pen
3. Live within limits
4. Be respectfully his

If you consistently yield to the Spirit's arrows in these four ways, there's no way you'll stay a Control Girl for long.

❁ As prompted by the Spirit, recall some Big Arrow corrections in your life.

❁ Have you yielded to the Spirit more in the Big Arrows or the Small Arrows? How has this affected your transformation?

For Meditation: Galatians 5:25

During the small moments of the day, I either gratify my craving for control or give control to God. *Holy Spirit, thank you for laying down arrows of guidance for me. Please remake me to be like Jesus as I yield, moment by moment, to you.*

Lesson 2: Tame Your Tongue
Read Ephesians 4:29–32; Matthew 12:33–37

THERE'S A REASON I chose the "tame your tongue" arrow first. The Bible compares the tongue to both a rudder on a boat and a bit in a horse's mouth. Like rudders and bits, my words create a direction for my life. Am I yielded to the Spirit, or vying for control? You'll be able to tell by the words streaming out of my mouth.

AM I CONTROLLING?

Once, as I was speaking on the Control Girl topic, a mother leaned over to her adult daughter and whispered, "Am I controlling?" Her daughter thought for a moment, and then whispered, "Yeah, you are." The mother, dissatisfied with this answer, settled back in her chair and listened to me say a few more things about Control Girls. Then, leaning back over to her daughter, she whispered, "I'm not like *that*, am I?"

The daughter hesitated, then whispered back, "Yeah, Mom. You are." The mother listened to me speak for a few more minutes, and then leaned over to her daughter once again, saying, "Really? You think I'm like *that*?"

The daughter, now exasperated, whispered, "Mom. You're trying to control me *right now!*"

I love how that story illustrates our own blindness to our problem with control. Sometimes, we don't even feel the controlling undertow of our words, but other people do. So here's a challenge: Ask a few people who love you most whether you have a Control Girl tongue. Ask if they ever sense you're trying to control them by what you say. But most of all, begin asking the Spirit of God to show you any undercurrent of control in your words.

WORD WEAPONRY

Our words are the primary way we try to control the people we love. We raise our voices, insert a sigh, ask manipulative questions, use an inflammatory tone, criticize, undermine, demoralize, and gossip.

And our electronic words add an extra zap of power. Like when a wife texts her traveling husband to ask if he's sleeping alone as her way of holding past sins over his head. Or a woman tweets about "some people" with one person in mind.

Given the effectiveness of words, it's no wonder we quickly resort to them, especially when we feel like we're losing control. Remember how Sarah attacked, Rachel demanded, and Miriam undermined? They each tried to control with words, yet in each scenario, words did not ultimately control the outcome.

The same is true for us. We can attack or cut people down, but this doesn't necessarily change the situation. We can use guilt or shame to manipulate, but we can't ultimately make others desire the same things we desire or do what we want them to do. We can spray words like bullets, but this only puts holes in our relationships and weakens our influence.

That's what happened with my dishwasher song. One afternoon, after I cleaned up the entire kitchen, I set a stray drinking glass on the counter. When I came back hours later, my glass had multiplied and had babies. There were now approximately thirty-seven new glasses, plates, and mugs on the counter.

My family members—all able-bodied and capable of placing dishes in the dishwasher—were scattered about nearby. So in a playful manner, I said, "Oh . . . I know what's going on here. You guys are *scared* of the dishwasher, aren't you? It's dark in there, and you're afraid the dishwasher monster might bite off your hand if you stick it inside. Is that it?" Everyone chuckled, understanding my implied message.

As I loaded their dishes, I sang a little song to the tune of "I'm not Afraid of the Big, Bad Wolf." Only I changed the words to, "I'm not afraid of the dish-wash-er, the dish-wash-er, the dish-wash-er . . ." I had winsomely delivered my message. My intentions were good. No harm done.

But a few days later, the same thing happened. One glass multiplied into dozens next to the empty dishwasher. This time, as I loaded, I wasn't nearly as playful or winsome as I sang, "I'm not afraid of the dish-wash-er, the dish-wash-er . . ." Sheepishly, several family members hung their heads. Someone said, "Sorry, Mom."

Then it happened again. This time I was mad. I bellowed, "I'm not afraid of the dish-wash-er . . ." and made sure my voice carried to the far corners of the house. This quickly became a habit. Every time I loaded their dishes, I sang the song. Rather than sweet and playful, I was snarling and rude. I sounded a bit like the big, bad wolf.

Then one day, I was convicted by Ephesians 4:29–30: "Let no corrupting talk come out of your mouths, but only such as is good for building up, as fits the occasion, that it may give grace to those who hear. And do not grieve the Holy Spirit." I had not been building up my family with fresh, encouraging words; I was using stale, rotten words to control them. But ironically, I had not gained control. I had sung the dishwasher song dozens of times with no effect. It only made everyone cringe and recoil. My dishwasher song was grieving the Holy Spirit, and it was time to stop. I wanted the Holy Spirit to control me instead.

Remember the Hold and Fold concept we discussed in chapter 1?[1] We have to Fold and give God control of the people who disappoint and frustrate us—sometimes every day. And we have to Hold control of ourselves, especially of our tongues.

OK . . . but how? I can walk serenely down from my bedroom, having just spent time with the Lord, praying, "Jesus, take the wheel. Let me be an offering to you," and then see some mess my kids have made and immediately blast them. I feel like Paul when he says, "I've lost control—sin has taken up residence in me and is wreaking havoc. . . . I can will myself to do something good, but that does not help me carry it out" (Rom. 7:17–18 VOICE).

The one who *will* help us carry out good is the Spirit of God. But **the Spirit doesn't act like a filter over our tongues; he changes our hearts, where our words are first formed**. Matthew 12:34 says, "For out of the abundance of the heart the mouth speaks."

TRAINING MY HEART

Years ago, I realized I had a habit of grumbling and being irritated with my husband throughout the day. I would find his brush left out, and growl, "*Grr* . . . Ken!" Or I would see the protein powder he spilled, and say, "*Tss* . . . He drives me crazy!" Or I would notice that the light-bulb was still burned out, and groan, "*Chh* . . . He still hasn't done that!"

In these little ways, I was training my heart. I built patterns by repeatedly giving vent to my desire to control Ken. Then when he came home in the evening, I would snap at him about forgetting the milk or not shoveling the driveway. I was disproportionately angry and critical. But after a day of fuming, it's just the way my heart was already inclined.

To change my words about the milk or the driveway, I needed to back up and yield my heart earlier in the day. It started with the brush, the powder, and the lightbulb. In *those* moments, I had to decide: Would I cave in to my desire for control or would I surrender control of my husband to God? Would I choose to grumble and fume or be grateful and cheerful? My choices set a trend. By training my heart, I form the words that will come tumbling out later.

As a Control Girl, words are the primary way I try to control people. But as a Jesus Girl, words are the primary way I give up control to God. Taming my tongue starts by yielding my heart in the small moments of the day. As I give the Spirit control, new words are formed—cheerful, gracious, kind words. Like a rudder, these words set a new direction for my life.

❋ Do others detect a controlling undertow in your words?

❋ How have your controlling words proved futile?

❋ How does privately fuming or venting with a desire for control set an inclination for your heart and words?

❋ Compare your tongue to a rudder. Where are you headed? What change is needed?

For Meditation: Psalm 141:3

Words are both a primary way I control people and a primary way I give control to God. *Lord, may my words today be formed by a heart that practices cheerfulness and gratitude rather than grumbling and fuming.*

Lesson 3: Cap the Red Pen
Read 2 Timothy 2:23–26

WHEN BETH WAS little, she and her sisters had to stay up on the couch until their dad got home from work. Their mom wanted him to see the vacuum lines in the carpet, which would get blurred if little feet were prancing about.

Then, after Beth was married, she found her mother-in-law on her knees one day, running her hands over the carpet. Beth asked what she was doing, and her mother-in-law said, "I just vacuumed, and I want to get rid of the carpet lines." What? Beth had been taught that carpet lines were the gold star of housekeeping! Who's right? Who's wrong?

As Control Girls, we can laugh about carpet lines. But when the stakes are higher, it's not so funny. When a son is about to marry the wrong girl, or a husband is about to take the wrong job, we're no longer asking who's right. We're telling who's wrong. We feel almost *obligated* to pick up our red pens and edit in our own version of a Happy Ending.

Mothers particularly have this sense of obligation. I heard of one mother who spoke up at a college orientation meeting, saying, "I'm paying for this. Shouldn't I get access to my daughter's online information? If I don't stay on her about her grades, she'll flunk out!" But the facilitator said, "Well, this is college. It's up to her now."

Once again, the Hold and Fold principle is helpful.[2] When our children are little, we must Hold little hands, or slap them away from danger. A good mom will repeatedly, and winsomely, correct her children. But good moms also eventually Fold and hand their red pens over to the Holy Spirit. Only the Spirit can convict at the heart level, which is where true course correction happens. **Capturing and correcting the hearts of people is God's business, not mine.**

INSTEAD OF LECTURING

A couple of years back, I hosted a "Five C Challenge" on my blog, inviting women to join me in twenty-one days of abstaining from any correcting, criticizing, complaining, condemning, or comparing.[3]

For me, not correcting was the hardest. A few days into the challenge, my third grader was notably disrespectful and rude as I fixed his breakfast. Ordinarily, this would have prompted a corrective session from me, complete with lecturing, Bible verses, and punishment. But this time, I was quiet. So quiet, you could hear the bagel sizzling in the toaster.

It popped up, and as I began to add butter, my son said softly, "I'm sorry, Mom. That was rude. Will you forgive me?" Amazingly, he hadn't needed my correction. He already knew what I was going to say. What he needed most was to hear the voice of the Spirit, which my lecturing may have drowned out.

Now, I'm not saying that we should always be quiet and wait for the Spirit's correction. Sometimes—usually out of fear—a mom consistently avoids correcting her child. Maybe she doesn't want him to get upset with her. Or she's not sure if it's right to step in. I heard about a teenage boy who wouldn't come downstairs for his own birthday party. He was up in his bedroom with his girlfriend, and his mom didn't want to interrupt. Well, my friend, that is not a time to wait for the Spirit to speak to your child. Parents who never correct their children are not keeping them close, as they might imagine; they are pushing them away—both from their families and from God.

So where is the balance? How do we know when to correct and when not to? The Spirit of God is our advisor. He guides us in a way that no list of parenting guidelines ever can. When we hand over our red pens in prayer, he guides our corrections, not just in parenting but in other relationships as well.

When I'm chomping at the bit, my fists full of red pens, I can be fairly certain that my inner Control Girl is leading. But when the Spirit is leading, I often *don't* want to correct the person. I dread it. In that case, my confrontation is offered out of obedience and concern for the other person.

CONTROLLING IN RED

Remember, anger and anxiety often bubble to the surface when we're trying to control. This is especially true when my red pen is in hand. During a fretting frenzy, I clutch my red pen with excessive criticism, focused on where this all might lead. In an angry rant, I wave my red pen at the offenses committed in the immediate past. Both my anger and anxiety signal a deeper struggle with control, which I might not readily see. My red pen is just the way I'm trying to *get* control.

Recently, with rather unfortunate timing, my son introduced some comic relief to a classroom discussion. His classmates laughed; his high school teacher didn't. Instead, she called my son to the front and embarrassed him. Then she held him after class, yelled at him, and threatened to drop him from the class.

The story brought my Control Girl blood to an instant boil. How dare she bully my child? This teacher needed to be corrected. She needed to see my perspective. It was my obligation to advocate for my son and students like him. So I went to work on an email, spilling *lots* of red ink.

I thought I was being helpful, but when my husband read it, he said, "Uh . . . that's not helpful." So I rewrote it, and again Ken said, "Yeah, that one's not helpful either." After my third draft, he said, "Shannon, this will make things worse."

I decided to call my friend Eric, who is a high school teacher. I said, "When a parent reaches out to you, do you find it helpful? Do you appreciate getting input?" Eric said that all teachers occasionally get emails filled with red ink, but a teacher's first line of defense is always, "Oh, it's just another crazy parent, trying to control."

There was a bit of silence on my end of the line. I said, "Can you repeat that?" I couldn't believe Eric used the word *control* . . . to the woman writing a book about controlling women! I got off the phone and thought, *He's right. I am trying to control.* I hadn't even realized it.

Had the teacher been disrespectful? Yes. But would my son survive the semester unscathed? I was pretty sure he would. So my red ink was fueled by a desire to control the teacher, and not necessarily to simply protect my son. I deleted all drafts of the email and relinquished control to God. If he stops the ocean at the sand and keeps the earth tilted and spinning, surely he's got my son's teacher under control without my help. Besides, no amount of red ink from me can accomplish what one nudge from the Spirit of God can.

Rather than frantically correcting and controlling, the Spirit wants me to quiet my turbulent soul. Psalm 4:4–5 says, "Be angry, and do not sin; ponder in your own hearts on your beds, and be silent. . . . Put your trust in the LORD."

If I'm gripping my red pen, I'm not trusting in the Lord. I'm trying to take control again. Throughout my day, each flutter of fear and jaw-clench of anger is another opportunity to retrain my heart. Every time I lay down the red pen and put God in charge of correcting people, I am the one who is changed the most. How can I go from Control Girl to Jesus Girl? Capping my red pen and quieting my soul is transformational.

✸ List the ways you are presently most tempted to spill red ink. Now ask God to prompt a heart change for each situation on your list. Date your requests, and watch for God to work.

✸ Take the Five C Challenge: go five days without correcting, criticizing, complaining, condemning, or comparing. Ask the Spirit to retrain your heart as you put the cap on your red pen.

For Meditation: 2 Timothy 2:25

Capturing and correcting the hearts of people is God's business, not mine. When I correct, I'm often trying to control. *God, I believe that no amount of red ink from me can accomplish what one nudge from your Spirit can.*

Lesson 4: Live Within Limits
Read Galatians 5:13–25

AUBURY'S HABIT WASN'T dangerous. It wasn't illegal. It was an activity you'd probably encourage your kids to do more of. Aubury was a reader. But reading had begun to take over Aubury's life. She was reading eight hours a day, then ten, then twelve. And even when Aubury was doing something for her young children, she wasn't truly present. Her mind was consumed with the characters in her books.

Aubury kept her reading a secret for a long time. When her husband noticed unfinished housework, she told him that mothering was overwhelming. (What guy can argue with that?) But then, one night after Bible study, everything changed.

Aubury unveiled her ugly habit to a godly woman from her group and shared how disgusted she was with the way reading consumed her life. The woman prayed over Aubury, begging God for freedom. And in that room, a quiet miracle happened. Aubury was set free. From that point on, Aubury gave up her excessive reading and experienced joy and freedom from giving God's Spirit control.

INSIDE THE LIMITS

More chips, another hour on social media, or another drink. Each seems to offer an escape from the harsh realities of life. So we stretch the limits, thinking that freedom comes from escaping control. Then our lack of self-control quickly leads to bondage.

The Spirit's arrows always point us back inside the limits. True freedom is found in exercising self-control, not in boundary-free living. So the Spirit gives us the power to say *no* to ourselves. We often don't experience immediate freedom from addictions like Aubury did. Healing can be a long process. But whether the Spirit's power is released instantly, or over a series of instances, it is God who sets us free to live within limits.

Notice how many limits God has woven into our daily lives. A day has twenty-four hours, no matter who lives it. A dollar has one hundred cents, no matter who spends it. And a donut has three hundred calories, no matter who eats it.

God built limits into our lives for the same reason he placed the tree in the middle of the garden. He wants us to relinquish control on a regular, ongoing basis. He wants us to find freedom and joy that come from living within limits.

Two Reactions

I find that, out of my love for control, there are two ways I react to limits.

Reaction one is to chafe against the limits and be irritated with them. It's when I say, "I don't care how many calories it has. I'm eating the whole thing." Reaction one causes me to struggle with my weight, my budget, or being anywhere on time. It's when I don't get enough sleep, watch too much TV, or eat junk food. Why? Because I hate the constraints of limits. I prefer indulgence and excess.

Reaction two is putting a stranglehold on limits in an attempt to achieve total control. Reaction two is all *about* limits. It's when I know exactly how many calories I've eaten today. Or when I'm stressed out because I only have two hours before bed and four hundred calories yet to burn. It's when I'm vigilant about taking vitamins, getting enough sleep, and being on time—and angry when I don't get the results I'm counting on.

So reaction one is when I *reject* limits out of a love for control.

Reaction two is when I *clutch* limits out of a love for control.

But God wants me to *relinquish* control. On the surface, response two might seem to be Spirit-led because it involves heavy doses of self-control. But there is a version of self-control that lacks patience, kindness, joy, and peace. This isn't the fruit of the Spirit; it's the fruit of a controlling heart.

Galatians 5 describes one fruit with many characteristics. We shouldn't picture a tree covered with various fruits, but rather one fruit (or one life) with all of the beautiful qualities listed: loving, kind, gentle, and self-controlled.

It's important to differentiate between self-control that says yes to *our* desire for control, and self-control that says yes to *God's* control. Reaction two might involve rigidly counting calories, pennies, and minutes—but not because we are relinquishing control; it's our way of *seizing* control. We want to be perfect, and control is the way we try to squeeze ourselves into that mold.

In contrast, Jesus Girls have a self-control that focuses on others, like Jesus did. Spirit-led self-control requires constant dependence on the Spirit as we learn to lean on his strength and not our own.

LIMITING HIS STRENGTH

It's ironic to me that the downfall of mankind was introduced by a woman and her food. Eve could have eaten any fruit but one, and that's the one she had to have. It's a control thing.

Recently I was convicted that eating is an area of life that I have roped off from the Spirit. I often ignore his arrows of conviction—usually with a bowl of ice cream in my hands. So, with a desire to retrain my heart to surrender to God's Spirit, I went on the strictest diet I have ever tried.

The first month went great. I was fitting back into jeans that had been collecting dust on my closet's top shelf. I was feeling more energetic and encouraged by my progress. But then, the weight loss slowed to a creeping pace. I was discouraged and started grumbling about the hamburgers and fries my family was eating (and sneaking a few fries myself). My self-control was running out.

I stepped on the scale one morning and started crying when I saw that the number had not budged for a whole week. I said, "God, I can't do this." Then I sensed him whispering, *That's the point.* How quickly I had forgotten that my goal was to retrain my heart, not just shed some excess pounds. God doesn't tell me to rely on myself for self-control. Rather, Galatians 5:16 says, "Walk by the Spirit, and you will not gratify the desires of the flesh."

I truly believe that God weaves limits into our daily lives for rigorous, ongoing heart training. He wants us to consistently be in the practice of yielding to him. Food will probably always be a struggle for me.

For you, it might be alcohol, spending, entertainment, sex, or something else. But little by little, day by day, as we yield to God's Spirit rather than our own cravings for more, we are set free. In the process, our controlling hearts are changed.

❀ Give an example of reaction one and reaction two from your life.

❀ Reread Galatians 5:13–25. Write down everything the verses say about freedom and the Spirit.

❀ What limits do you sense God offering as a way to train your heart? How could God use these minute-by-minute limits to turn you into a Jesus Girl?

For Meditation: Galatians 5:16

Godly self-control is the fruit of the Spirit, not a product of my perfectionism. God weaves daily limits into my life as training for my heart. *Holy Spirit, please use the limits I encounter today to cultivate in me an attitude of surrender.*

Lesson 5: Be Respectfully His
Read Ephesians 5:15–33

IN HER BOOK *For Women Only*, Shaunti Feldhahn says that women typically want to control things, and husbands perceive this as disrespect.[4] I know my young husband did.

When I nagged about his eating habits, he heard me question his judgment. When I spoke for him in social settings, he heard my lack of confidence in him. When I yanked the bedsheet out of his hands because he was putting it on sideways, he saw disrespect and disdain. By repeatedly trying to control every little detail, I sent inherent messages of disrespect to my husband. And even when I did it subtly with soft, little irritated sounds, I communicated in full volume, "I can't trust you to do anything right, and I'm disappointed and frustrated with you."

Poor Ken. He didn't deserve any of that. He's actually quite fabulous. He's hardworking, generous, compassionate, and witty. He's a kind daddy and a faithful husband. But I think Prince Charming himself would have given me cause to roll my eyes. The problem was not with my husband; it was with me.

UNDER THE INFLUENCE

Ephesians 5:33 says, "Let the wife see that she respects her husband." Most wives, I think, would readily agree with this verse. Wives *should* respect their husbands. We just don't see our behavior as disrespectful.

My wise pastor says, "Sin always feels like sin when it's done to us. But sin rarely feels like sin when we're doing it to someone else."[5] So when a husband is lazy, irresponsible, selfish, or unfaithful, this *feels* like sin to his wife. But when she emasculates, dishonors, or disrespects him by taking control, it rarely feels like sin to her. It feels like she's reacting to legitimate complaints.

A wife can go on indefinitely, never seeing her disrespect as sin. And even if she does recognize disrespect as sin, how can a wife be genuinely respectful toward a husband she's struggling to respect?

Thankfully, God's Word has an answer. In Ephesians 5, if we back up a couple of paragraphs from that instruction to respect our husbands, we see several ideas clustered together: "And do not get drunk with wine . . . but be filled with the Spirit . . . submitting to one another out of reverence for Christ" (Eph. 5:18, 21).

Remember that being filled with the Spirit is like being under his influence. We do things we ordinarily wouldn't—like submitting, or putting ourselves second. In our flesh, we only put someone first when they've earned our respect. But the Spirit prompts a wife to submit out of reverence for Christ, not necessarily for her husband. So under the influence of the Spirit, a wife puts Jesus in control of her marriage. She does this by respectfully deferring to her husband rather than trying to control him.

OVERDUE RESPECT

There was a day, about a decade ago, when God showed me my sin of disrespect. My friend Angela was visiting when I happened to find a random library book shoved way under the couch. I wondered aloud whose book it was, and Ken said, "Oh, I think I checked that one out with the kids . . . a while ago, maybe?"

I instantly realized that *this* was the book causing our fines to accrue. Looking pointedly at Ken, I said, "OK, from now on *you* are not *allowed* to check out library books! If you can't be responsible, you can't check them out!" I'm sure my expression read, "You're an idiot."

Looking back, what now seems most telling is how quickly I dismissed this. I moved on with the day's activities without the slightest feeling of remorse. I didn't interpret my attitude toward Ken as disrespectful or rude. I had just taken control and set things straight, just like I always did.

But that evening, Angela called and said, "Shannon, God really convicted me when I heard you talk to Ken about that library book. I realized that I sometimes speak to my husband that way too. I wondered if we could pray for each other that God would help us respect our husbands as we should."

I asked if I could call her back. Even though Angela didn't have a "red pen" demeanor, I was initially embarrassed and humiliated. But as I evaluated myself with newly opened eyes, God's Spirit broke into my heart. Angela was so right. My disrespectfulness toward Ken was ugly and wrong. I called her back with remorse over my sin. And I asked Ken to forgive me as well, not just about the library book interchange but also for the sinful patterns of disrespect that had taken root in my heart.

God used a friend and a library book as a Big Arrow in my life, pointing out my ugly, controlling heart, and my overdue need for change. I shudder to think what kind of wife I'd be today had I never begun inviting the Spirit to lay down new arrows of respect for my husband.

The influence of God's Spirit is powerful. Can you imagine the potential for transformation over decades of marriage when a wife chooses to repeatedly respect her husband rather than control him? Over time, as I yield to the Spirit, God is changing me from a Control Girl into a Jesus Girl.

❀ How do you control your husband? How does this communicate disrespect?

❀ How can you encourage other wives to be respectful of their husbands?

❀ Ask for the Spirit's conviction. Pray for the Spirit to influence you to be genuinely respectful.

For Meditation: Ephesians 5:33

By trying to control my husband, I send inherent messages of disrespect, which might not feel sinful to me, but are. *God, out of respect for you, I will treat my husband with respect today.*

Your Happy Ending

IN THIS BOOK, we've mined the stories of seven Control Girls in the Bible, looking for lessons on control, ourselves, and God. As we've combed through their stories, we've seen that clamping down on control creates anything but the Happy Ending we were envisioning. And surrendering to God brings the peace and security that lunging for control never can.

In closing I'd like to share one more story about a woman in the Bible. But instead of another Control Girl, this woman is a beautiful example of a Jesus Girl.

Mary was in the middle of planning her wedding when she learned that a baby was coming. If ever there is an event a girl wants control over, it's her wedding. And if ever there is a situation sure to shatter her illusion of control, it's an unplanned pregnancy.

In Mary's day unwed mothers were outcasts. Their communities shunned them and their would-be husbands left them. So this news of an unexpected pregnancy was no small matter. A baby would change everything for Mary.

Yet when Mary learned that she was to conceive God's Son by the power of the Spirit, did she erupt in anger? Did she have a panic attack? No, she said, "Behold, I am the servant of the Lord; let it be to me according to your word" (Luke 1:38).

Do you hear the beautiful surrender in Mary's words?

Now, I can't say for sure, but I'm guessing this isn't the first time words like these fell from Mary's lips. Most likely, during the months and years leading up to this point, she had been cultivating a heart of surrender—inviting God to use her life however he chose. So when the angel showed up with the cast list for God's unfolding drama, Mary almost seemed to be expecting him. When she saw her name next to the role "mother of God's Son," she didn't scoff or faint or scream. She was sweetly willing.

We've watched so many women in the Bible contend for their own small-minded plans and purposes with no regard for God's plans and his bigger, more thrilling story line. We've seen them clutch their illusion of control with sweaty, frantic hands. We've watched them fool-ishly wreak havoc, convinced that vying for their version of a Happy Ending was worth the heartache and struggle. But, oh, what a beautiful contrast Mary offers! With only a moment's notice, she gave up control over her life. She entrusted her body, her reputation, her relationships, and her future to the big, wise hands of God. Mary chose to serve Jesus with her life, and what a blessed life she had.

This is the sort of woman I want to become—a Jesus Girl. It's what I want for you too. My hope is that we will be women who cultivate hearts of surrender, ready to say at a moment's notice, "I am the servant of the Lord; let it be to me according to your word."

And now it's time to go! We can't wait until tomorrow. Today we must start, in big ways and small, to give control to God. He is ready and willing to rescue us from our Control Girl ways and lead us to the most satisfying Happy Ending imaginable.

Notes

Introduction: My "Happy" Ending

1. John Piper, "Manhood and Womanhood: Conflict and Confusion after the Fall" (sermon transcript), *Desiring God*, May 21, 1989, http://www.desiringgod.org/messages/manhood-and-woman hood-conflict-and-confusion-after-the-fall.

Chapter One: Path of a Control Girl

1. Dee Brestin, *Idol Lies* (Brentwood, TN: Worthy, 2012), 18, 74.
2. Timothy Sanford, *Losing Control and Liking It: How to Set Your Teen (and Yourself) Free* (Colorado Springs: Focus on the Family, 2008), 60, 62, 70.
3. Scott O'Malley, conversation with the author, Jan. 28, 2015.

Chapter Two: Eve

1. Mary A. Kassian, *Girls Gone Wise in a World Gone Wild* (Chicago: Moody Publishers, 2010), 122–23.
2. John Piper, "Manhood and Womanhood Before Sin" (sermon transcript), *Desiring God*, May 28, 1989, http://www.desiringgod.org /messages/manhood-and-womanhood-before-sin.
3. Karen Neumair, email correspondence with author, May 22, 2015.
4. Susan Foh, "What Is the Woman's Desire?" *Westminster Theological Journal* 37, no. 3 (Spring 1975): 376–83.
5. Raymond Ortlund, "Male-Female Equality and Male Headship," in *Recovering Biblical Manhood and Womanhood*, eds. John Piper and Wayne Grudem (Wheaton: Crossway, 1991), 97.
6. Ibid.

Chapter Three: Sarah

1. Robert Alter, *Genesis: Translation and Commentary* (New York: W. W. Norton & Co., 1997), 68.
2. Bruce Waltke, *Genesis: A Commentary* (Grand Rapids: Zondervan, 2001), 253.
3. Scott O'Malley, email correspondence with author, May 21, 2015.
4. Timothy Keller, "Sarah and the Laugh," *The Timothy Keller Sermon Archive* (New York: Redeemer Presbyterian Church, 2013), accessed through Logos Bible Software.
5. W. A. Criswell, ed., *Believer's Study Bible* (Nashville: Thomas Nelson, 1991), note on Gen. 25:31, accessed through Logos Bible Software.
6. "Five Reasons Millennials Stay Connected to Church," Barna, Sept. 17, 2013, https://www.barna.org/barna-update/millennials/635-5-reasons-millennials-stay-connected-to-church#.V28y7bgrLIU.

Chapter Four: Hagar

1. Bruce Waltke, *Genesis: A Commentary* (Grand Rapids: Zondervan, 2001), 254.
2. Ibid., 296.
3. Jim Samra, "Pride and Humility," Calvary Church audio podcast, accessed May 22, 2015, http://calvarygr.org/sermon/pride-and-humility/.

Chapter Five: Rebekah

1. Timothy Keller, "A Con Artist's Struggle," *The Timothy Keller Sermon Archive* (New York: Redeemer Presbyterian Church, 2013), accessed through Logos Bible Software.
2. Timothy Keller, "The Problem of Blessing," *The Timothy Keller Sermon Archive* (New York: Redeemer Presbyterian Church, 2013), accessed through Logos Bible Software.
3. Timothy Keller, "Wrath: The Case of Esau," *The Timothy Keller Sermon Archive* (New York: Redeemer Presbyterian Church, 2013), accessed through Logos Bible Software.
4. Emerson Eggerichs, *Love and Respect* (Brentwood, TN: Integrity, 2004), 235.

Chapter Six: Leah

1. Erin Davis, *Graffiti: Learning to See the Art in Ourselves* (Chicago: Moody Publishers, 2008), 29–30, 56.
2. Timothy Keller, "The Struggle for Love," *The Timothy Keller Sermon Archive* (New York: Redeemer Presbyterian Church, 2013), accessed through Logos Bible Software.
3. Ibid.
4. Bruce Waltke, *Genesis: A Commentary* (Grand Rapids: Zondervan, 2001), 404.
5. Keller, "The Struggle for Love."

Chapter Seven: Rachel

1. Paula Hendricks, *Confessions of a Boy-Crazy Girl* (Chicago: Moody Publishers, 2013), 17–18.

Chapter Eight: Miriam

1. R. Dennis Cole, *Numbers: An Exegetical and Theological Exposition of Holy Scripture*, The New American Commentary (Nashville: Broadman & Holman, 2000), 200.
2. Nancy DeMoss Wolgemuth, "Willful in the Wilderness," *Remember Miriam* DVD (RightNowMedia.com and Revive Our Hearts, 2012), www.rightnow.org.
3. Dan Wright, email correspondence with author, Feb. 24, 2015.
4. Ibid.

Chapter Nine: Control Girl to Jesus Girl

1. Timothy Sanford, *Losing Control and Liking It: How to Set Your Teen (and Yourself) Free* (Colorado Springs: Focus on the Family, 2008), 60, 62.
2. Ibid.
3. Thanks to Hilma Conklin for sharing these with me!
4. Shaunti Feldhahn, *For Women Only: What You Need to Know About the Inner Lives of Men* (Sisters, OR: Multnomah, 2004), 26.
5. Jeff Manion, personal conversation with author, Mar. 5, 2015.

About the Author

SHANNON POPKIN loves to blend her gifts for humor and story-telling with her passion for the truth of God's Word. Shannon speaks for Christian ladies' events, retreats, and moms' groups—encouraging women of all ages to put their hope in God. You can connect with Shannon on her blog (ShannonPopkin.com), Facebook, Twitter, Instagram, and Pinterest. Shannon is also a regular contributor for the *True Woman* blog at ReviveOurHearts.com.

Shannon is happy to be sharing life with Ken, who makes her laugh every single day. Together, they live the fast-paced life of parenting three teens. When she's not taking pictures from the sidelines of her kids' sporting events, Shannon loves to be home, opening her front door to friends and family.

A free small group guide and a sample set of meditation cards are available for download at www.shannonpopkin.com